CANCER IS FUNNY

Keeping Faith in Stage-Serious Chemo

JASON MICHELI

D0873468

Fortress Press
Minneapolis

To Dennis for showing up
To Ali, "For better, ~~For Worse~~"
To the people of Aldersgate, for never telling me to
make effing lemonade

CONTENTS

INTRODUCTION: CANCER IS FUNNY

I unbutton my shirt to expose a chest so smooth it would've been the envy of the pimpled boy who came home from gym class and, after thumbing through his contraband *Sports Illustrated: Swimsuit Edition,* shaved off the dark hair breaking out all over his chest—and other places. He used his mom's pink razor, with a blade so dull it had left a line of rust on the soap tray in the shower. Like that sixth-grader, who suffered the urgency to fit in with the boys whose bodies were not yet outpacing the sex ed syllabus, I long to look and feel normal again.

I mention this irony to S—, my nurse. She smiles.

It's hard to make someone blush who wears rubber gloves for a living, but when you're a clergyman and everyone presumes your occupation makes you officious and tight-sphinctered, it's not so difficult to make them laugh.

I add to S— how my mother had no idea when she gave me a *Sports Illustrated* subscription for Christmas that one day every year, the *Sports Illustrated: Swimsuit Edition* would arrive in the mail like Charlie's golden ticket. "I don't know how many afternoons I spent thumbing through that *Swimsuit Edition* . . . with my left hand," I say, and she snorts a little and laughs, freely, as though if God is in a place of suffering like this, then the surest sign of him or her is our laughter.

I tell her how I'd never confessed to the shaving before (or to the being my own best friend), at least not until I got cancer. She nods, understanding how, with cancer, every moment feels appropriate for a confession.

I spread my shirt at the collar to give her access to the dual rubber tubes of my chest catheter into which, one week per month, the chemo-poison drips and from which today, like nearly every day, my blood gets drawn. I watch how it comes out like cheap boxed wine, cab-colored and with a slightly foamy ring around it. It splatters against the plunger of the syringe that's twisted onto the end of my catheter, and I think, as I often do, how the tubes in my chest port resemble the nozzles on a life preserver, the kind they stow underneath the seat on airplanes.

What would happen, I wonder, if sitting there in the infusion center among so many elderly patients, I suddenly pretended to panic and blow into the ends of my catheter as though it were a life preserver? How many of them would realize that they were not, in fact, on an airplane and were unlikely to crash-land or drown? I smile at the thought as S— draws the last of my blood and then squirts it into the third of her vials labeled with my name and date of birth, and then I imagine the commotion as confused seniors claw and push each other out of the way, vainly searching out parachutes and oxygen masks before bravely hurling themselves over the counter and through the beveled glass of the nurses' station window. They're not called the Greatest Generation for nothing.

I chuckle at the picture playing out in my head. "What's

so funny?" she asks, gathering up the empty syringes, used alcohol wipes, and spent gloves.

"Funny? I was just thinking that next time I unbutton my shirt here, I should sway my hips a little and go Da, Da, Da, Dum." I get an eyebrow from her and a crack about sexual harassment claims on top of my medical claims. "Good point," I concede. "Besides, you wouldn't want to get complaints from all the elderly women here that you'd led them to expect a special screening of *Magic Mike* during their chemo infusions." She snorts again and laughs. I wouldn't wish such laughter upon my very worst revenge fantasy enemy.

The laughter, coming easily and without a need for explanation, suggests we both know, even without saying it, that being deadly serious here of all places—especially here—is the surest way to feel seriously dead already.

CANCER F@#$ING SUCKS

I can get away with saying cancer f@#$ing sucks even though I'm a pastor, because everyone, as I soon learned after my diagnosis, knows cancer f@#$ing sucks. Every family tree has the C-word carved angrily into some part of it. Now that I have cancer, I notice how I rip the scabs off the wounds everyone seems to carry.

Everyone knows that cancer f@#$ing sucks.

The only way for doctors to save your life, just as Jesus warned, is to bring you as close as possible to losing your life without actually killing you—though I doubt that poison derived from mustard gas was what he had in mind. No matter how many celebrities wear lapel ribbons, many cancers, such as my own, have no cure, and chemotherapy can provoke all sorts of unpleasant side effects, including—I kid you not—cancer.

If the sentiment expressed by the 753 sympathy cards I now keep in a taupe Sterilite box is any clue, then everyone already knows it: cancer f@#$ing sucks. It's why no one knows what to say to you when they find out you have cancer. It's why everyone is afraid to ask what it's like to have cancer. And it's why, since no one knows what to say and everyone's afraid to ask, when you find out for the first time you have cancer, all you know is that it's going to suck. And make you throw up.

But here's what I want you to know if you or someone you love has cancer:

Cancer is funny, too. No, wait, it really is funny.

Any ailment that results in pubic-hair wigs being actual products in the marketplace simply is funny. (They're called merkins. Look it up.)

For example, on my third day of chemo, I gripped my sutured stomach like a running back desperate to hold on to the pigskin, swallowed a mouthful of nausea, and dragged myself and my wheeled chemo pump into the bathroom of my hospital room in order to clean my toilet before the shy Muslim housekeeper could arrive to clean it.

The TV in my hospital room had been running a feeding-frenzy loop of coverage on Islamic terrorism and the fear it engendered in the West and among Christians. Given the violence in the Middle East and the rising specter of fundamentalisms, Christian and Muslim, the least I could do for the cause of peace, ecumenical understanding, and Jesus Christ's kingdom (these were the actual thoughts in mind) was to wipe my own diarrhea stains from the toilet. *There are already enough reasons in the world for hatred and bloodshed between us besides my chemically induced squirt stains all over the toilet,*

I thought to myself, as I dragged my traction-socked feet over the bed.

When she found me next to the toilet on the bathroom floor, unable to pick myself back up, and asked what I'd been doing, I told her.

"Jesus said, 'Blessed are the peacemakers,'" I said with an almost straight face. She laughed so hard that she had to adjust her hijab.

When I first found out I had stage-serious cancer, I thought my family and I had laughed for the last time. Thank God, I was terribly, totally wrong. Cancer f@#$ing sucks, sure, but cancer's funny, too.

During the summer, in the middle of my treatment, I joked to a nurse that considering I'd started to wear a straw fedora to protect my baby's-butt bald head, and since their front desk offered lollipops in glass bowls, I should start greeting all the nurses with my best Kojack: "Who loves you, baby?"

She countered that the show had been off the air so long I'd probably just send the wrong message by calling the nurses "baby." I'd now be the lecherous priest they had as a patient.

"You know how Telly Savalas died, right?" she asked.

I shook my head.

"Cancer."

She waited a beat before she let the smile begin to crease around her eyes.

Then we both laughed.

WHAT'S SO FUNNY ABOUT CANCER?

Cancer is funny. I don't mean the ha-ha that only fills awkward silences. Nor do I mean the kind of humor that's intended to parry conflict, avoid confrontation, or escape the trading of hard truths—habits of humor I've been trying to unlearn since I got married.

When I say cancer is funny, I don't have in mind the sort of funny that allows you to keep wearing your mask and the lies that have grown up to fit it. I'm not referring to the jokes that make it possible to glide over eggshells unbroken, comedy I began practicing soon after my dad showed up to my basketball game with what my friend described as "a funny smell on his breath." I couldn't yet make a layup, but I could've already lettered in (self-) defense, dissembling and distracting from my shame and pain with humor.

I don't mean cancer is funny in that way—although, because cancer is scary as hell, there are plenty of laughs like that to hide behind.

No, when I say cancer is funny, I mean that your every pretense falls away, right along with your pubic hair. It makes you absolutely vulnerable to others, both to their fragile, pitying stares and to their sincere gestures of support you would've proudly shrugged off before cancer.

Cancer refuses to let you stand at a comfortable adjacency to life.

It announces your mortality—our species' number one subject of avoidance—in a style as ugly and obvious as a spray-on tan or title loan sign.

Cancer leaves you with no other choice but to trust the last people you would choose to trust: others. Whether you're throwing up in your friend's car or hearing the checkout clerk doubt aloud that the driver's license photo is really you, once the malignancy is found in you, there's no way to hide, and hiding the ugly bits of ourselves is a human preoccupation. With no way to hide, there's no longer any reason to pretend. Your false self falls away.

The spoonful of sugar that comes with all this medicine is laughter. It's not a kind of laughter to be confused with happiness. I have stage-serious cancer; I'd be crop-circle crazy if I were happy about it. Instead it's a laughter that feels like . . . joy, a laughter that can trace the line between disaster and the farce that we call life, feeling not well or strong but free—genuinely free—to be myself, with others and before God.

Really, that's the biggest joke cancer plays on you.

It renders you no longer resembling yourself. Your blood chemistry merely confirms what you already suspect, that you're only a partial version of your former self, yet simultaneously you're more your true self than you ever were before cancer. I didn't expect to find this kind of laughter in the cancer ward.

People attribute it to Mark Twain, but it was the comedian, Steve Allen, in a *Cosmopolitan* article in the 1950s, who said:

Comedy = Tragedy + Time

What makes laughter possible, according to Allen, is the cushion of time smoothing the rough edges off an unhappy ending. Comedy requires twenty-twenty hindsight. Time—as in "time heals all wounds"—has to dispense its medicine and do its magic before the saltiness of tears can give way to even saltier humor.

Most cancer patients, however, don't have enough time removed from the shock of their diagnosis to laugh at the disease. Indeed, many fear, as I know only too well myself, that they don't have the remaining time they'd always thought they had, and without time, it's damn near impossible to laugh.

But now that I've had Death sniff me over good, I question whether Allen's theory of comedy should enjoy maxim-like status. Just as it is in space, I've discovered that time is relative in the shadow of the valley of death. When tragedy dings over the Doppler of your family's dreams and your only fear is how much time you have left, you discover that everything about the time you do have gets condensed. Concentrated. Distilled down to the percentage of proof that warms more than it burns.

As it turns out, you don't need the cushion of time to laugh, because stage-serious cancer is like the end of *2001: A Space Odyssey*. There's no kettle drum accompaniment with cancer, but you do feel your entire lifetime being lived every instant, as though the measure of you is being taken at each moment. One side effect of this experience is that you receive each day as a gift no less precious than the sum of them.

CANCER = COMEDY IS RELATIVE TO TRAGEDY

Still, with cancer, the grace of each day doesn't stop you from retracing all your steps leading to today, stopping along the way to rehearse your every delight and your regrets like an actress with butterflies on opening night, examining every episode of your story to see if it yields a meaningful thesis. The tragedy-plus-time formula makes humor seem like simple arithmetic: an unhappy ending plus the safety of distant memory equals comedy. But in the shadow's valley, time is relative. Who you are and who you've been and who you might (not) be are always ever before you, and as crowded as that sounds, it creates room for laughter. For when you don't know if tomorrow will come, there's no need to save face for it.

Thus, cancer can be funny because belly laughs are easier when you're not crouched down in a defensive posture.

———————

They write out my chemo schedule by hand each month, scribbling the names of my drugs on different days in a curly hybrid of print and cursive, before making photocopies and handing one to me. The schedules can prove hard to read, which I pointed out to my oncologist a while back: "What's this prescribed on my schedule for Friday, Saturday, Sunday, and Monday?"

"Ah, that's a *d*. It says 'dex.' It's short for dexamethasone."

"Funny, I thought it looked like a lowercase *s*," I said, feigning disappointment. "You might have to apologize to my wife. I already showed this to her and said, 'Doctor's orders.'"

He pretended not to hear me, staring at my labs on the computer screen, before replying. "Well, if you could pull that off four days in a row after six months of chemo, then I really should get you into a clinical trial. You're worth studying."

He looked down at me across the bridge of his long nose, the way he does when checking my chemo-lacerated mouth for sores. I smirked. "You stole my punch line," I said, and for a moment at least, our mutual laughter muffled the hushed echo of bad news being broken in the adjoining exam room.

LAUGHTER BY SUBTRACTION

A trick that was once popular among comic magicians is called the Disappearing Dove. The performer would cover a supposed dove with a white handkerchief and then "release" the bird into the ether. Only, in this bit, the handkerchief would just fall to the ground and lie there, still, not moving, not flying away, not disappearing, not a dove at all.

Not only do I think Steve Allen was mistaken about the necessity of time for comedy, I believe he erred in seeing tragedy as the only soil in which laughter can be sown. Sometimes what makes something funny, painfully funny, isn't the punch line but what's missing—the absence of something we've grown to count on and expect, your status no longer being quo.

Obviously, so much of what you experience with stage-serious cancer is just this sort of absence—an absence of health, obviously, but even more critical, an absence of hope. There's the vanished libido (kidnapped by chemo) and the missing-child milk carton reflection ("Have You Seen Me?") in the mirror, gone right along with the innocent, untroubled look in your children's eyes and your leaky bucket list.

Absence.

Like the showers you used to take with your wife, now replaced by sponge baths and baby wipes, a trade-off that seems to strike at the very heart of the wedding liturgy's "for better/for worse" yin-yang and strikes you as weightier even than the sudden downturn in your personal futures market. With cancer, you feel no more *you* than a dove that's not really there; you name that bird your new normal, and—all the predictable rage and sorrow aside—that can turn hilarious.

Comedy, contrary to Allen's math, doesn't always have to be the sum of tragedy and time. Sometimes it's a matter of simple subtraction, of being minus some part of your life, of suffering the difference between what was and what is left. Let's set up another equation for that:

Comedy = Your Life − _____

Fill in the blank with something or someone you've taken for granted.

It goes without saying, but laughter by subtraction is necessarily more personal than time added to tragedy. Like my grandpa, who for years managed my grandma's fading memory (he used to joke, "What's the best part of Alzheimer's? You get to hide your own Easter eggs!"), those who can find the funny in absence are those who feel most acutely what's missing.

Maybe that's why it's surprising to hear cancer can be funny. The laughs must come from those who've got it.

Then again, maybe humor isn't about addition or subtraction. Maybe comedy has a different source than time or tragedy, absences or unhappy endings. Maybe cancer is funny not because of what you suffer or how you suffer it, but because of who else is there with you as you suffer in the cancer ward.

Ever since I first used Google to search for *mantle cell lymphoma* and discovered I have an exceedingly rare lymphoma that *almost always* affects only men in their old age (as in, not thirty-seven year olds. Dumb luck that caused me to chuckle—after crying like a man-baby), I've wondered if the surprise that cancer is funny has less to do with how we conceive of the disease and everything to do with how we understand the nature of the Divine. I've wondered because the most common questions I've received during my treatment are all about God.

They're not even veiled questions. Cancer is just the excuse to drill down and inquire about the existential:

- "How has cancer deepened your faith?"
- "Have you grown closer to God in your suffering?"

True, I'm a minister, and my line of work tends to invite such conversation, but talking with other patients, these kinds of questions are par for the cancer course. Even when the question is phrased in the negative, as in "How has struggling with cancer challenged your faith in God?" the premise still connects the experience of suffering with an experience of God. Implicit in such questions is an assumption first asserted by John Chrysostom, a fourth-century Christian clergyman whose oratory netted him the nickname John Goldenmouth.

He wasn't always the flawless orator.

Proving that a golden mouth does not guarantee a gem of a mind, Chrysostom once preached, "Tears bind us to God, not laughter." For that sermon's text, Chrysostom could've turned to the Gospels, because the four evangelists do not ever record that Jesus laughed. John tells us that Jesus wept, and Mark depicts a *Fight Club* Jesus going at a fig tree. Matthew and Luke join the other two in reporting Jesus' temple tantrum, but none of them ever mentions that Jesus laughed. Not once. Not at anything. Or Chrysostom could've also had in mind Saint Paul, the early church's equivalent of a killjoy chaperone at your junior high dance. Paul, in several places in his letters, admonishes the faithful against silliness, joking, and laughter.

As a pastor, I can attest that you need only walk into any church on a Sunday morning to find Christians earnestly abiding Paul's admonishments, not only in their humorlessness but, more generally, in the way they privilege seriousness over laughter and do not regard humor as a spiritual discipline. After all, grim, penitential introspection, not levity, marks Lent, the most spiritually significant season of the church year. Saint John of the Cross got famous by writing about the dark night of the soul, not the bright, happy daytime.

You might expect to find such esteeming of seriousness and suffering in a religion with a cross at the front of every sanctuary and an execution at the heart of its story, but the Gospels frame their narratives not from the perspective of the crucifixion, but from the hindsight of resurrection's happy surprise. In other words, the laughter of Easter, not the laments of Good Friday, should determine for us how we conceive of God and ourselves as God's creatures.

LAUGHING THROUGH THE CRUCIBLE OF CANCER

Everyone assumes that suffering leads the sufferer to God, and sometimes it does. Suffering can knock down all our other (self-) defenses so that we can finally, wholly, depend upon our maker. But if suffering leads us closer to God, suffering should not leave us mirthless.

Pierre Teilhard de Chardin, a French philosopher and priest from the twentieth century, posited as a sort of first principle, "Joy is the most infallible sign of the presence of God." The first time I heard my youngest son's belly laugh,

I marveled over how a celibate like Pierre had understood about God what it took fatherhood to teach me.

Everyone assumes suffering leads you closer to God. And no one registers surprise to hear how cancer has led someone to a deeper (i.e., more *serious*) faith, but people betray something like shock when you suggest to them that cancer can be funny. If God is Joy, then we can't rightly be said to have grown closer to God, through suffering or any other means, without a marked increase in joy, and with joy comes laughter, mirth, and a levity only the good news of grace makes possible.

Despite the finality with which he expressed it, John Goldenmouth Chrysostom was only partially correct. Tears, and the suffering that provokes them, can in fact bring us closer to God by leaving us no other options but turning to God. But tears and suffering cannot fetter us to God. Only joy can bind us fully to the God who is most infallibly Joy.

Cancer is funny, then, because the suffering occasioned by cancer draws you nearer to God, and the closer you get to God, the louder laughter becomes.

After I was diagnosed with cancer—a cancer that makes my death no more certain than yours, but likely much more proximate—I received dozens of books: cancer books. Many of them offered practical diet and exercise advice that promised to improve my odds of living. Other books announced themselves as spiritual and, in a nutshell, exhorted me to have faith that I was being watched over by a God who knew every hair on my soon-to-be-balding head. The former type of books all lacked the existential wrestling that's as much a part of cancer as nausea, while the latter betrayed none of the gritty emotional honesty that I believe separates faith from kitsch.

None of those books prepared me to anticipate what I found to be true: that cancer is funny.

Not only is this book a no-bullshit take on what it's like to journey through stage-serious cancer and, in turn, struggle with the God who may or may not be doing this to you, I hope this book will help you or someone you love laugh through the crucible of cancer.

After eight cycles of nine chemo drugs, I believe laughter is still the best medicine, but even more so, I've come to believe laughter is the surest sign you're not alone, because joy is the most unmistakable indication of God's presence.

A teacher of mine, Robert Dyktra, once told me that the ancient Jews believed our God-implanted, eternal soul was stitched in our gut, actually located in the liver. I'd wager they believed this because that's the part of us that hurts the most when we laugh.

CHAPTER 1.

I THOUGHT I HAD CANCER

So I thought I had cancer, just in time for Christmas. A few weeks before my kids unwrapped their presents under the tree, the dermatologist unwrapped me underneath the soul-killing fluorescent lights of his office park suite. I thought I had cancer, but I didn't really. I guess I should start the story there.

THE HAIRY MOLE IN THE MANGER

I and my wife, Ali, became preoccupied with the idea I might have cancer in November. For weeks, I was obsessed with an image of me in a stocking cap, knit by someone who couldn't bear the notion of a world without me in it, looking as stoic as a character in a Sylvia Plath poem.

I had this mole, you see, on my right shoulder.

It wasn't gross or anything. It was just large and discolored, and it had a few hairs growing out of it. "Suspicious," my former-premed spouse called it, and then she'd point at it and quote that line from Uncle Buck about finding a gutter rat to gnaw it off.

Ali had been after me for months to go to the doctor

and get it checked out. But because I'm an idiot, instead of going to the doctor, I consulted WebMD, a website (I'm now convinced) that was designed by terrorists to frighten Westerners. If you haven't checked out WebMD already, *don't*. It's the most terrifying corner of the Internet you'll ever browse.

I consulted WebMD for a suspicious mole, and twelve hours later, I logged off in black despair, convinced that I suffered from IBS and TB, convinced as well that my kids have ADHD and maybe scoliosis to boot, and that I might as well preorder those little blue pills, because "that" is likely right around the corner for me as well.

To be honest, even though I spend two or three hours every day admiring myself in the mirror, I didn't even notice the mole was there. I didn't realize it was there until that summer when I took my shirt off at the pool and Ali threw up a little bit in her mouth.

Normally, me taking my shirt off at the pool is an Event (with a capital *E*), a moment that provokes jealousy among men, stirs aspiration among boys, and awakens fifty shades of Darwinian hunger in women. Like Bernini unveiling his *David*, normally me taking my shirt off at the pool is a siren call, overpowering all reason and volition and luring the primal attention of every female to be dashed against this rock.

But I digress.

The point is, when I took off my shirt at the pool that summer and saw my beloved wipe the vomit from the corner of her mouth, it got my attention. Ali got after me to go to the doctor. My youngest son, Gabriel, who tried to biopsy my mole for his new microscope, got after me. My mom, who is a nurse, got after me. And the voice in my head confirmed what WebMD and all the rest had told me.

But my personal philosophy has always been that if you wait long enough, the worst will always happen, so for months and months, I didn't do anything about it. Then, one behind-closed-doors kind of night, Ali whispered across the pillow that she was never going to touch me again until I scheduled an appointment.

I called the doctor the next morning.

Of course, because I have health insurance, I couldn't just call the dermatologist to schedule an appointment. No, that would make us communists. First I had to blow a morning and a copay at the general practitioner in order to get a referral to the skin doctor.

The nurse at the general practitioner's office weighed me and, with a tollbooth worker's affect, took my blood pressure. Even though I told her I was just there for my mole, she insisted on typing my age into her tablet and asking me the questions that my age automatically generated.

First question: Have you experienced depression or thoughts of suicide in the past month? Her second question was "Have you noticed an increase in memory loss recently?"

"Not that I recall," I said.

Stone-faced, she moved on to her third question, asking for the date of my last prostate exam. "Uh, never," I stammered, and not sensing my sudden anxiety, she asked me when I'd had my last colonoscopy.

"Wait," I said, "I'm not old enough to need those things done, am I?"

"Just about," she replied.

"In that case, can we go back to the depression question?"

Ten days and three double-billing mistakes later, I went to the dermatologist, clutching my referral like a winning lotto ticket.

When I last went to the skin doc in 1994 as a puberty-stricken middle schooler, his office was one step above the guy who showed up at gym class and told you to turn your head and cough. This time around, it felt like something from the Capital in the *Hunger Games*.

I walked into the steel and glass, Steve Jobs–like office, where a receptionist with impossibly purple hair and a dress made of feathered, bedazzled boas handed me paperwork on a clipboard and told me to have a seat. "All I Want for Christmas Is My Two Front Teeth" was playing overheard while a flat-screen TV on the wall advertised the dermatologists' many services that do away with age, imperfection, and garden-variety ugliness. A slide advertising the office's newest service, eyebrow implants, slid horizontally across the plasma screen.

Judging from the model's face on the screen, eyebrow implants are a procedure designed to give septuagenarian Realtors Tom Selleck mustaches above their eyes. The next slide was a photo of the office itself, along with its staff, centered above a cursive catchphrase. Their mission statement: "Feel as perfect on the outside as you do on the inside."

As I filled out the paperwork, I wondered what sort of psychotic person came up with a slogan like that. I mean, if their goal was for me to appear on the outside how I normally feel about myself on the inside, then I'm already as ugly as I need to be.

Bruce Springsteen's "Santa Claus Is Coming to Town"

started to play as a door opened and a nurse, who looked a little like the supermodel Elizabeth Hurley, called for Mr. Michelle. Nurse Hurley led me through a maze of hallways to a room so antiseptically bright I half expected to be rendered into Soylent Green.

Inside the exam room, Liz handed me a hospital gown, instructed me to take off all my clothes, and promised that the doctor would be there in a few minutes.

"*All* my clothes?" I begged for clarification. "Yep, even your underpants," she said.

For some reason, Liz Hurley using the word *underpants* on me made me feel like a five-year-old boy whose mother makes him follow her into the ladies' room. She closed the door gently behind her as I unfolded the baby-blue gown.

Now, as a minister, I've spent a lot of time in hospitals, but at that point, I'd never been a patient. Most of the patients I had seen had been underneath sheets and blankets. Holding my own hospital gown in hand, I suddenly discovered that the correct way to wear it is not as self-evident as you might think. *Are you supposed to wear it open in the back, like cowboy chaps? Or should you wear it open in the front, like a bathrobe?*

"Or maybe," I pondered aloud, "you should take your particular ailment as a guide." Since my mole—the cause of my visit—was on the front of my body, I reasoned, I should opt for the latter style. So there I sat, like The Dude in *The Big Lebowski*, sans White Russian in hand.

And I was naked.

If I was unsure about the correct way to wear the gown, I got my answer when the doctor knocked, entered, immediately snorted, and said, "Oh, my."

"I wasn't sure . . . ," I started to explain, but he waved me off. "It's OK, not a problem. You won't have it on for long anyway." Words that proved to be more auspicious than temporal.

"Are you cold?" he asked, looking at me. "We can turn up the heat."

"No, I'm fine."

The doctor sat down on a round stool in front of a black computer, and I proceeded to give him my professional diagnosis based on my education from WebMD. He listened and rolled his eyes only once when I told him I suspected having MS in addition to cancer, and when I finished, he said, "Let's have a look."

So I showed him my mole, which—I'll point out—was very easy to do, since I was sporting the gown like a smoking jacket.

He looked at it for a few moments, looked at it through a magnifying glass for a few moments more, and then, just as Rod Stewart started to sing out in the lobby "Have Yourself a Merry Little Christmas," the doctor said, "I don't think there's anything to worry about. The hairs growing out of it just make it look worse than it is."

Relieved, I started to get up to get ready to go, but the doctor said, "Not so fast. While you're here, we should probably do a full body scan."

"We?" I wondered to myself as he left and returned a moment later with Liz Hurley, who—I noticed—struggled to suppress a giggle when she saw me in the gown.

With Liz gawking, he proceeded to peel back my gown like it was cellophane on a side of beef, which is probably a good analogy, because there's nothing quite like being naked, perched on top of butcher paper, clutching your bait and tackle, to make you feel like a piece of meat—that grayish, 50-percent-off, sell-by-today ground round.

The date-rapey Christmas song "Baby, It's Cold Outside" started to play, which seemed appropriate, since they then both bent me in impossible positions as though I were a yoga instructor or Anthony Weiner on the phone. Bending and contorting me, they picked over my every freckle and blemish as if we were a family of lice-ridden mandrills.

"Anything suspicious *down there?*" he asked ominously.

"I hope to God not," I said, but apparently invoking the Deity did not provide sufficient medical certainty for him, because he took his examination south, which was when he decided—for some reason—to ask me what I did for a living. Normally, when strangers ask me my profession, I lie and, invoking George Costanza, tell them I'm an architect. It helps avoid the awkward and endless conversations that the word *clergy* can conjure. But with no clothes on and even less dignity, there seemed to be little reason to pretend.

"I'm a minister," I said.

"Really? What tradition? You're obviously not a rabbi," he said with a wink.

"I'm a Methodist minister," I said.

"My grandmother was a Methodist," he muttered.

Maybe it was because the whole situation was so impossibly awkward, but once I started talking, I found I couldn't stop. You'd be amazed how interesting you can make denominational distinctions sound when you're in the buff and being pawed over like a 4-H cow.

I could hear John (Cougar) Mellencamp's "I Saw Mommy Kissing Santa Claus" as the doctor finished and said in a measured tone, "You do have some moles on your back we should remove. Don't worry; none of them look concerning."

Then he ordered me to sit back down and lean forward as far as I could, which I did, clutching the last corner of my gown against my loins. The doctor took a black sharpie and drew circles on my back, which struck me in the moment as not very scientific; meanwhile, Liz Hurley grabbed a digital camera off the supply counter.

Under normal circumstances, the combination of supermodel, a nurse's outfit, and a digital camera would pique my interest, but somehow I knew what was next.

She told me to lean forward again so she could snap some close-ups of my back, which she did with slow, shaming deliberation. Then (I can only assume to degrade me further) she actually showed me the close-ups of my back. Now it was my turn to throw up a little in my mouth.

"That's what I look like from behind? It's like a flesh-colored Rorschach test. I should call my wife and tell her I love her," I said.

She laughed and said, "The images are magnified, so don't worry. Trust me, everyone appears kind of ugly and gross when you get up that close for a look."

"And that's not even the ugliest part about me," I said.

She frowned. "Do you think there's something we missed?"

"No, no, you were thorough all right," I said. "I was just thinking of my soul."

"I guess that's your specialty, huh, Father?" Liz laughed. The doctor laughed, too. They thought I was joking. They both thought I was joking.

James Taylor was finishing his rendition of "Lo, How a Rose E'er Blooming," singing the line that goes, "True man, yet very God, from sin and death he saves, and lightens every load," as I sat on the butcher paper and watched Liz load the snapshots of me onto the black computer. Watching each unflattering image first pixilate then load onto the screen in front of me, I thought again of that cursive catchphrase in the lobby and what rubbish it was: "Feel as perfect on the outside as you do on the inside." If you could get close up—all over—to me, not just looking at my skin but living in my skin, living my life—and not just in my shoes but in my flesh—then you could come up with many more ugly, indicting pictures of me than a hairy mole.

The cold, incarnate truth is this: I'm even more pockmarked and blemished on the inside than I will ever appear on the outside.

On the inside, I'm impatient and petty. I'm judgmental and a liar. I'm angry and insecure and fearful and unforgiving and—and I'm just a normal guy. If you stripped me all the way down, not just of my clothes but of my pretense and prevarications, stripped off the costumes I wear and the roles I play right down to my soul, then you'd see how unsightly I really am.

I pretend.

I act like everything's all right when it's not. I pretend me and mine are happy when maybe we're not. I act like I've got my shit together even when it's falling apart all around me. I project strength when I feel weak, and I wear other people's projections of me like masks. I don't keep it real. I pretend. I play-act. I hide. Just like, I'll bet, you do.

You can get by with such bad but passable habits so long as nothing too terrible, in terms of challenges, comes your way. I had always gotten by before.

Over the speakers, I could make out Aretha Franklin belting out, "Hail, hail the Word made flesh, the Babe, the Son of Mary," from the second verse of "What Child Is This?" As Aretha sang and Liz finished up with my snapshots, the doctor gave me a patently false promise about not feeling a thing just before he started to dig out my first mole with the finesse of a mobbed-up Italian barber from North Jersey.

"Sorry," he apologized. "Maybe it's not numb enough." With the gentleness of a cycloptic, differently abled butcher, the doctor removed the rest of my blemishes and finished up. "You should come back in a year, so we can do this again."

"I can't wait," I said as I started unfolding my street clothes. Dressed, with my back looking like Clint Eastwood's in *Pale Rider*, I found my way back to the lobby.

Hearing Aretha overhead, seeing my snapshots on the computer screen, and thinking of my shame that morning and every unsightly truth it brought to mind, I thought of Saint Gregory of Nazainzus, the fourth-century mystic who taught that what it means to say "God was in Christ" is to say that all of our humanity is in the God who was in Christ.

All our humanity. Every bit of every one of us. It has to be.

Otherwise, as Gregory put it, "That which is not assumed is not healed." Those parts of humanity not taken on by God in Christ are not healed. Those embarrassing parts, those imperfect parts, those shameful and fearful and broken parts of us—if it's true that Christ comes to save *all*, then all those parts of us are in him; otherwise, they're not healed.

Every bit of every one of us is in him, Gregory said. So there's no need to hide. There's no need to wear masks or put on brave faces. Everything that scares us silly we can give over to Christ, because it's already in him. We're not perfect on the outside, and we don't need to pretend that we are on the inside, because every part of us is in him already.

It was a good nugget of wisdom to recall, because even though I'd just been given a clean bill of health from the dermatologist and, in truth, had never seriously feared I had cancer, what lay ahead of me was scarier than anything I'd read on WebMD.

I left the doctor's office silently thanking God to the sound of carolers singing, "Cast out our sins and enter in, Be born to us today," from "O Little Town of Bethlehem."

When I got home that night, I felt the first of what would be daily, doubled-over, distractingly painful stomachaches. I should've seen them coming. I'm not implying causality necessarily, but a God who works by empty tombs is a God who just loves surprises.

BEING HANDED A SACK OF SHIT

The Christmas carols had fallen off the radio weeks earlier when Ali and I walked into that very same medical building in late January. Unlike before, there was no joking this time. The apprehension was real. Holding our breath the way we used to do in the pool with our son Gabriel before reciting together, "Ashes, ashes, we all fall down," we rode the elevator down a floor below the dermatologist's office to a surgical suite.

In the waiting room, I held Ali's hand as tightly as I had on our wedding day. I was terrified—we both were terrified—of the space we occupied in that moment, the pregnant pause between "in sickness and in health." At that point, I'd performed around seventy weddings. Only there in the waiting room did I finally notice how the church's vows always lead with the expectation of sickness.

My gastrointestinal doctor had called me the evening before, a Thursday evening already dark with winter. Apparently bedside manner doesn't apply to phone calls, for as soon as I answered my cell, the doctor hit me with the most clichéd and inauspicious of greetings.

"Jason, hi, it's Dr. P—. Are you sitting down?"

WTF?

"I'm looking at the results of your scan. Are you sitting down?"

I gulped a yes.

"You're not driving, are you?"

"No," I lied.

The soft but unmistakably real concern in his voice belied the clumsy manner in which he queried me, both of which combined to make my heart beat the way it does on a roller-coaster when it teeters at its apex, giving you a glimpse of the bottom just before gravity does its work.

And we all fall down.

In fact, I was driving when he called. It was my night to man the swim practice carpool, and heading back to our neighborhood, I was listening to my boys and their friends talk about girls only half-jokingly for the first time. I was expecting the GI doctor to call (but not tonight—why was he calling tonight?!) and tell me I suffered from gallstones or ulcers or some benign if painful nuisance that would end in a familiar suffix.

Blank-itis, I was expecting to hear.

I guess not.

Earlier that morning, I'd driven—one-armed and bent over my steering wheel, gripping my stomach from the stabs of pain—to a nondescript office. It was the sort of office space you see thrown up hastily in con movies, with just enough decor and detail to fool the mark. An order from the GI for a CT scan lay on the passenger seat next to me.

Then, at the office, the bottles of berry-flavored barium they made me drink contradicted every signal my belly was busy sending me. I writhed on the waiting room sofa underneath a TV screen, where a muted *Good Morning America* played while I swallowed the barium down in sips and waited for my name to be called.

Before the scan, the CT tech told me brusquely to drop my pants and then, as a kind of apology, tucked me into my mechanical bed with a warm blanket. Afterward, he told me that I shouldn't expect to hear anything of the results for a few days. "Sometime early next week," he said as I buckled my belt and stared at the manhole-shaped camera that had whirled around my bowels. "Maybe Tuesday or Wednesday you'll hear something from your doctor—no earlier than that," he said with a reassuring absence of alarm.

Since the start of Advent, I'd chalked up my abdominal pains to too much coffee in my stomach, too much fat in my diet, or too many church people in my schedule. Only my wife knew I was suffering such pains, a fact I attribute to my off-the-charts virility.

The cleanses and abstentions by which I attempted to remedy myself did nothing. By New Year's, the pain had grown, and grown so regular, that dinners with church members felt like the scene in *Syriana* where a fat George Clooney gets his fingernails removed by masked terrorists. Whenever I jogged, it felt as though I were carrying something hot and heavy in my colon, dropping my weekly mileage from thirty miles per week to none at all.

Heartburn. It's got to be heartburn, I told myself every time I had to walk back home. Then, unable to sleep, I spent an increasing number of nights on the sofa slurping fro-yo for sustenance and binge-watching entire seasons of *Californication.*

Still, I held it as a kind of defeat when I surrendered to Ali's commonsense pleas and scheduled an appointment with my general practitioner.

"I feel like Harry Dean Stanton in the first *Alien,*" I replied when she asked me to describe the pain.

The doctor blushed when I added, "And I hope you're my Sigourney Weaver."

When initial blood tests yielded no answers or even clues, she ordered a workweek's worth of stool samples to see if I was carrying more than the usual stowaways in my gut.

Clutching her order, I marched across the office park parking lot and into the cramped box of a LabCorp office that still would've had the seedy feel of a meth lab were it not already crowded with prospective employees praying that the previous night didn't show up on their urine tests. The receptionist sat approximately four inches from the knob of the entry door, a malevolent-looking woman filing her nails as an excuse, I deduced, to avoid eye contact. I was close enough to braid her hair; it took determined effort for her to ignore me, which she did. Only the chorus of Billy Ocean's "Caribbean Queen" greeted me when I stepped inside.

I stood there until Billy Ocean faded out and into

Duran Duran before I finally coughed and said, "Um . . . excuse me, miss? I've got an order here from my doctor."

She started filing the fingers of her other hand without sparing me a glance. Her nails, I noticed, were bejeweled with topaz-colored stones and stickers of the Tasmanian Devil.

"You've got to sign in," she declared with the sort of measured exasperation you hear from nurses in senior centers.

I looked around. "Where do I sign in?"

She sighed. Clearly I was a prodigal who'd spent a lifetime disappointing her. "On the clipboard," she said, still filing away.

I looked around. "Um, where is the clipboard?"

She finally looked up and looked around, and rolling her eyes in tandem with her swiveled chair, she grabbed the clipboard from the countertop behind her.

"Sign in and take a seat," she told me, flashing a demonstrably fake smile.

I looked around. The five seats were all filled. Indeed, the entire waiting room felt like all of Ellis Island had been squeezed into a model living room at IKEA. Masses huddled, waiting on the floor. I joined them there on the ground and waited until my butt cheeks grew numb, when the receptionist finally called me forward. I handed her the order from my doctor, and she responded by opening a rusty filing cabinet drawer, retrieving a brown paper sack, and thrusting it at me.

I left the office and found my car. I didn't peek inside the bag before pulling out of my parking spot. Why would I? Ali was standing in the driveway when I pulled up to our house. I handed her the brown bag and wondered aloud how I was going to poop into such small plastic cups.

"I mean, my aim's good, but it's not that good," I said, handing Ali the bag.

"Ugh. Jason, there's stool in here."

"Yeah, I know, I've got to collect it for like a week."

"No, I mean there's someone else's stool in there."

I looked down inside the brown bag and gagged. The handwriting on the plastic containers was illegible, but, judging from the smudged name, I'm pretty sure whomever the poo belonged to was Asian. The samples floated in cloudy water in a way that momentarily brought my son's betta fish to mind.

"Throw. It. Away."

"Are you kidding?! I don't want this in our trash can."

So I drove it back to LabCorp with what was, I'll concede, not a little glee and self-satisfaction. And because I definitely didn't want it spilling in my car, I buckled the seat belt around the brown bag next to me.

When I returned to LabCorp, I threw open the door like a left-for-dead gunslinger swinging open the saloon gate, the setting sun obscuring his vengeful features. I let the winter air blow into the waiting room, but the receptionist was still filing her nails, and still she did not look up at me.

"You've got to sign in," she said with a malevolence so thick I wouldn't have been surprised to discover she was sitting on a pile of gold.

"On the clipboard," she added.

"Yeah, I *really* don't think I do have to sign in," I replied.

She raised her eyebrow and her hackles before she raised her head. "Oh, you don't think so, do you?"

"No, not really."

"And why not?" she asked, sounding eager for the challenge.

"Yeah, you gave me someone else's stool," I said matter-of-factly for the masses still huddled on the floor to hear.

"No, I most certainly did not." I couldn't tell whether she was disgusted or offended by the suggestion.

"I'm pretty positive. I didn't come back to enjoy your charming personality. Here, take a peek."

She covered her mouth. "I wonder how long that's been in the filing cabinet," she whispered into the brown paper bag.

"And I was wondering who didn't get that job they applied for because you left their stool samples in there," I said sweetly.

I could've sworn I smelled sulfur when she glared back at me. I made sure to check inside the second brown bag she gave me before I drove home, back to wondering how I was going to poop into those tiny plastic cups.

Even then I should've felt an inkling of what lay in wait ahead of us, because hearing you've likely got cancer feels *exactly* like a witch with a capital B handing you a sack of shit that doesn't belong to you.

FEELING VAGUELY SLUTTY

The following week, after my stool samples shed no light on what my doctor had started to call my "condition," I was sent to an ultrasound center for a look at my abdomen.

I hope that sounds as ridiculous as it felt: an ultrasound center.

Affecting the same deliberate look of uninterested non-attention I adopt whenever I walk past a lingerie store (or buy tampons for my wife), I grabbed a pink clipboard and a chair at the ultrasound center. At eight in the morning, there were already four other patients in the waiting room, and by patients, I mean, of course, women. All of them carried various-sized baby bumps, and all of them were accompanied by husbands or boyfriends—fathers to be.

I was the only single person there that morning, which left me feeling vaguely slutty. Or ashamed. Definitely, as I said, ridiculous. While I may have moobs, as my boys like to poke fun, I resembled none of the breastfeeding women in the artful black-and-white photos framed and mounted on the walls.

Evidently, a single guy at an ultrasound center was judged to be as awkward for the pregnant women in the room as it was for me, because quickly a nurse appeared and called my name before any of the others ahead of me in the queue. She had spiky yellow hair and a bread maker's hands. She led me down a hallway I'd seen once at a resort spa and led me into a darkened room filled with barely audible smooth jazz.

"That's baby-making music," I remembered Will Ferrell quipping in the first *Anchorman*, causing me to chuckle out loud.

The nurse responded by gruffly telling me to undress and lie down.

Shouldn't we chitchat a little first? I thought about saying. *I don't even know your name.* Instead, I did as I was told.

She squirted a long shot of hot jelly across my belly, which for me—as I'm sure it does for all the female patients—conjured compromising memories that seemed eerily prescient for such a place. Next, she rolled what looked like a handheld mixer over my middle and examined the Rorschach blot it produced on the adjacent computer screen.

"If you see a giant tapeworm swim across the screen, just seal-club me to death with that thing," I said.

She didn't laugh. I hadn't expected her to laugh.

"If I told you what I think I see, I could lose my job," she said flatly. "The radiologist has to read it and then forward a report to your doctor."

"But . . . you'd tell me if . . . something looked . . . wrong, right?"

"Nope, not my job. You'll have to wait to hear from your doctor."

"But—wait, does that mean there's something to hear from my doctor?"

"Not necessarily. I couldn't say either way," she said.

"But . . . if you saw something that was, like, urgent, you'd tell me, yes?"

"No."

"We're all done," she announced and tore off her latex gloves.

She stood up, and from the doorway, she threw a hand towel at me. "Wipe off and put your clothes back on," she said, equal parts clinician and Miss Kitty.

"Should I just leave the money on the table?" I asked with a straight face.

She didn't laugh at that either.

She didn't laugh, I've come to suspect, because she knew but couldn't say that I was, if not pregnant, carrying something inside me that would upend my life.

Then again, maybe she just didn't think I was funny. Maybe she didn't see anything on the ultrasound screen. The radiologist didn't. Neither did my doctor, who referred me on to a GI doctor.

THE SCARY WOODEN ANUS

Another week, and this time I sat in the GI doctor's exam room, staring at a terrifying wooden model on his desk of an anus and all its potential ailments.

"I've really got to stop eating shrimp with the shells on," I said to the empty, aluminum-colored room.

Dr. P— knocked and entered, neatly dressed and softly pleasant. Save for height, where he was lacking, his resemblance to Maury Povich was real, and so seemed his interest in my work and family. Eventually, he got around to asking me about my family history, what I ate and how much I drank, and any other symptoms I might have noticed. Finally, he asked if I'd lie down on the table so he could examine my "tummy."

Kneading the place where my six-pack used to be, he asked, "How long has your spleen been enlarged like this?"

I don't even know where my spleen is, I thought and looked over at the wooden anus on his desk. "Um, it's always been that way, I guess?"

"Would you mind unbuckling your pants so I can feel your groin area?" he asked, and immediately I started hearing in my head the late-night Cinemax music that had been playing at the ultrasound center.

"Sure," I said, pretending this wasn't awkward at all.

"How long have you had these lumps here on your groin?"

"What lumps?" And he took my hand in his and placed it on the spots. They felt like mothballs or gumdrops. There were three or four of them, just below my hip bones, on both sides of my body.

"I hadn't noticed," I said, feeling the way I do when the vet tells me my dog is years behind on her shots.

"Do you have any others like these?"

"You know," I said, "I do have this lump that appeared on my neck not too long ago." I pulled back my collar to show him a gelatinous-looking spot.

He felt around my neck and head. "There's some lumps on the back of your head, on your neck, as well."

And like a Jedi Master in whom the Force is strong, I could sense Ali doing a face palm and shaking her head over me, her idiot husband.

Still, I didn't think anything of the lumps. The idea that I could have cancer—really have it and not just kvetch about a hairy mole—seemed to me unbelievable. I was young and healthy. I exercised religiously, and speaking of religion, if being a pastor came with any job perks, then being exempt from things like cancer had to be one.

Before I could even button up my jeans, Dr. P— told me he was sending me for a CT scan.

And that's how, one morning, a bearded tech told me without any sense of urgency that it would be "several business days" before I heard anything from my doctor.

Except the doc called me the same night, long past closing time.

————————

"We don't see this very often—maybe once a year at most. Usually we only find it in very small children, and then we only find it because the pain is such that they cry uncontrollably. But in adults, we don't. . . ." His voice trailed off as I put the car into park in our dark driveway.

"Even now, I'm debating whether I shouldn't just send you straightaway to the ER."

"What?" I asked. "What don't you normally see in adults?"

"According to your CT scan, Jason, your tummy pain is caused by what's called an intussusception."

"A what?"

He spelled it for me, as though that answered my question. I lost a few letters in the shoddy cell signal.

"It's where part of your intestine invaginates into another section of your intestine."

"Vaginates?" I asked, confused.

"Vaginates? We learned about vaginates in Family Life," my eavesdropping son, Alexander, whom we call X, wondered from the passenger seat, just as confused as I was.

I covered the phone and whispered to him, "Why don't you and your brother go inside."

"It's where a part of your intestine folds back into itself, like the eyepiece of a telescope," the doctor explained.

"I see. Is it serious?"

"Yes, very," he said quickly. "It could cause a complete blockage, cut off the blood supply to the rest of your intestine, or tear your rectum."

I thought again of the wooden anus in his office.

"The real question is what could be causing the intussusception." His voice took a step lower.

"What does cause it?" I asked, sure the answer would be something along the lines of "not chewing your food properly" or "eating too many gas station pork rinds."

"In children, the cause is generally unknown, but in adults, typically . . . it's a . . . ummm . . . tumor that causes it."

All of a sudden, I was in a malignant version of *Jerry Maguire*. He had me at the word *tumor*.

I'm sure whatever else he said next wasn't superfluous, but I didn't hear any of it. I didn't hear anything. It was like someone turned down the volume and tuned in the video.

I pictured the photos of my Uncle Jim that traced the ascent of his parents' staircase when I was a boy about my boys' ages. In the photos, Jim had thick, black hair and hard muscles. Near the landing, there was a photo of him lifting weights and another of him in his high school wrestling uniform, his chin strap unbuckled beneath a broad smile.

I pictured those photos, and I pictured the GI Joe figures arranged on my bedroom carpet before me when my mom came in one day to tell me Jim had leukemia. I pictured, too, sitting on those same stairs when Jim came home after a long absence in the hospital and how I didn't recognize him—at all—with his chalky bald head and Halloween frame.

Jim was the first person I knew to die.

He was the first thing I thought of when Dr. P— laid the specter of the C-word on my lap. Thinking of Jim, I pictured my boys seeing me the way I'd seen him, looking like a shadow of someone else's former self.

And then, of course, I pictured my boys not seeing me. Ever again.

The C-word, I discovered, does that to you.

"I've made an appointment for you with Dr. C— for first thing in the morning. She's an abdominal surgeon. If the pain gets any worse tonight. . . ."

"I'll go to the hospital," I promised, wondering if he could hear the fissures cracking my normally cocky baritone.

When the doctor hung up, I called my mom first. I felt

I absolutely had to be able to tell Ali, "The doctor thinks I have a tumor," without crying or sounding scared shitless. I needed someone on whom I could practice breaking the news. My mom, who all along had supposed that perhaps I'd picked up a parasite in Central America, held out hope that it would prove to be nothing more. Next, I called my friend Dennis, who said, "I'm so sorry," and asked, as I'd hoped he would, if he could stop by later.

Neither telling my mom nor telling my friend steeled me sufficiently to call Ali, who was working late, to break the news. Perhaps because I'd done so very rarely in our marriage, she could tell I'd been crying. She got up to shut her law office door, and after I told her, she sniffed, "I'm coming home now."

I've no idea how long I sat in the car after we said good-bye and "I love you"—long enough for the inside of the car to grow cold.

I got out and stood in the driveway and let the winter air dry my tears before heading inside, where my boys were drawing their baths. Gabriel had locked the front door as a prank. I fumbled to get my key in the lock. My hands were shaking.

Cancer is funny.

But none of us laughed that night.

DO YOU BELIEVE THIS?

Ali and I met with the surgeon the next morning. Given her hasty and frank demeanor, neither of us was surprised when she told us she'd been an army surgeon. My surgery had been scheduled for first thing Monday morning, she said. She explained my procedure by taking a black Sharpie and drawing on the butcher paper rolled across the examining table.

Her artistic skills had me hoping she was better with a knife than a pen. Her illustration of my invaginated intestine appeared, even to my wife, distractingly phallic. It took up so much space on the butcher paper that I was left feeling flattered, despite probably having cancer. So striking was the phallic resemblance that every time Dr. C— used the word *cut* in describing my surgery and gestured to the drawing of my intestine, I winced and protectively grabbed my crotch.

Reading my file, she asked if she could check the lumps on my groin that Dr. P— had noted in his report. I said sure, stepped up to the examining table, and straddled a giant cartoon of what looked like my dingus.

"When I was in the fifth grade, my best friend's older brother had a magazine with a picture like this in it," I joked.

Ali shot me a look, so I refrained from pretending to wave a hat above my head while I rode a bucking bronco.

It tickled some as she traced along my pelvis before announcing to the room, "Yep, my money's on lymphoma," and then adding, cryptically, "That's good for me. We'll biopsy that while we're in there."

"In there?! In *me*, you mean."

She smiled, as if I were silly.

"Well, I'll see you Monday morning. Have a great weekend!"

And as quickly as she'd come, she left, and just as quickly, Ali's eyes started to tear. "My money's on lymphoma," Ali mouthed in shocked, mock cheer.

"What exactly is lymphoma?" I inquired of the picture of my penis on the exam table.

Ali laughed. The laugh came out easier because of the sob she'd been holding back. She wiped her eyes and smiled. She knew I was only half joking but that what I knew about lymphoma wasn't any more detailed than the sketch on the butcher paper.

Ali's smile got us as far as the elevator, where months earlier I'd been relieved to hear I didn't have the cancer I never really feared I had. It was just a hairy mole, I knew then. And now the smart money was on lymphoma.

Before we left, though, a nurse handed me a baby-blue folder with my name written on a torn piece of masking tape stuck on the front cover.

Cancer's funny.

Sitting at my kitchen table later that day and staring at the top sheet of paper in the folder, labeled "Preparations for Your Surgery," I didn't dwell on my own death, as I would've wagered, not immediately at least.

Instead, I first thought of all those other departed whose funerals I've officiated. So many that I know all the words of the liturgy by heart. Well over a hundred times, I've stood in the center of a sanctuary or in the middle of a funeral home chapel or at the head of an open grave on the fake plastic grass under an uneven tent or even a few times in a sitting room, and in front of all number and manner of mourners, and I've recited verses as inextricably linked with my character as "It is a tale told by an idiot, full of sound and fury, signifying nothing" belongs to the chorus of *Henry V*.

My lines, if not bald-faced lies or pious candy, signify a great deal more than nothing: "I am the resurrection and the life. Those who believe in me, even though they die, yet shall they live, and everyone who lives and believes in me will never die."

Sitting there in my kitchen, staring at the "Preparing for Your Surgery" memo with my surgeon's frank army countenance ("We won't know what we're facing until after your surgery") ringing on repeat in my head, it suddenly occurred to me that in all those times, I've never once stood by the dead and looked out at the living and proffered a follow-up question:

Do you believe this?

Cancer is funny. The question had never even occurred to me until my own death became something less than what my trade calls "speculative theology."

Do you believe (any of) this? That Jesus is the resurrection and the life? That those who trust in him (even though they die) yet shall they live? Are these just lines? Do you believe it? Really?

Now, sitting at my kitchen table, probably with cancer, I couldn't think of a more important question.

I'd never before thought to ask it, for one practical reason: the *United Methodist Book of Worship* doesn't instruct me to ask it. For another, very intuitional reason, it would seem boorish.

Funerals, after all, are mostly emotionally bare (as in vulnerable, not sparse) occasions with a higher likelihood of truth telling breaking out than during the rest of the workweek. And if the Pew surveys and Gallup polls are to be reckoned accurate, then the priest or pastor who dares to ask, "Do you believe this?" should be ready for roughly half the grieving gathered to answer, "No."

No, we don't.

We don't believe much of any of this.

In fact, I'd bet that the number of those responding in the negative would increase, the closer you crept to the front pews, especially on those occasions where the caskets are shorter or the left behind's hair less gray, those occasions where circumstances still seem to demand the wearing of black or where the shoulders are stooped not from age but grief.

I bet, if I asked, I'd hear more noes up close near the front. And so I'd never asked the question because neither my ecclesiastical script nor good manners suggest I do so.

Jesus does, though, in John 11, after speaking the lines whence my funerary script gets lifted.

The dead Lazarus's sister Martha gives the Gospel's best example of tearing Jesus a new asshole: "If you'd only come when I called, Jesus, my brother would still be alive."

Jesus responds with a resurrection rejoinder that ends where I begin whenever death enters in: "I am the resurrection and the life."

And then Jesus, unlike me, follows up with the question: "Do you believe this?"

Maybe, like Jesus, I should ask it too, propriety and piety be damned: "Do you believe this?"

Because, obviously, it's a question meant for the living. Jesus isn't asking what Lazarus believed. He's four days dead, serene and sealed in the tomb; nobody cares anymore what Lazarus believed. Not God. Definitely not Lazarus.

No, Jesus is asking Martha what she believes.

When Jesus tells Martha about the power of the resurrection, what Martha doesn't get is that Jesus isn't talking about a power available to us after we die. He's not talking about one day down the road or even about the Last Day.

He's talking about a power available in the present, today, in the here and now, because if you believe that Jesus Christ has destroyed Death, then resurrection doesn't just make heaven possible, it makes a bold life possible, too. If you believe that Death is not the last word, then we have the power to live fully and faithfully. And we don't have to try to live forever.

Here's what hit me only at my kitchen table, even after all those funerals: when you're staring at a euphemistically hued folder from your surgeon, and when the C-word has made a grim if hopefully premature intrusion into your not-yet-graying life, and when wildly melodramatic Lifetime-movie-type voices chatter in the back of your head, you don't much give a damn about forever.

Longer is all you want. Longer will do.

And here's what you notice, what I noticed: Martha's "Yes, I believe" doesn't guarantee a happy ending for her brother. The size of Jesus' tears outside Lazarus's grave suggest that even Jesus was a little shocked that the dead guy walked out newly alive, but even after all the trouble, Lazarus will die again—of old age and natural causes, or post-op infection perhaps, or maybe of a broken heart.

Martha says, "Yes, I believe," and no doubt she does. But seen from Jesus' point of view, she doesn't grasp at all what it means to believe, not any more than any creature can ever really comprehend her Creator.

She and Jesus are speaking past one another. He's talking about his very nature; she's talking about the Last Day. Even our strongest beliefs barely scratch the surface of what's True-with-a-capital-*T*.

In case those first two observations strike you as dissatisfying, here's the last thing you notice while staring at a baby-blue folder embossed with the caduceus and your name in hasty marker: A God who works by resurrection is, by definition, a God of surprises—light from darkness and all that. And a God of surprises is, by definition, *not* a genie in a magic lamp.

The antonym of resurrection isn't death; it's predictability.

Perhaps then that's the best reason not to add to the familiar script and pose that question to mourners: "Do you believe this?"

Even when the answer is in the affirmative, even where the faith is as strong-if-uncomprehending as Martha's, "Yes" is still a complicated answer. Now that the ~~shoe~~ gown was on the other ~~foot~~ body, I sat at my kitchen table feeling regret over any of the times in all those funerals that I might've implied anything other.

CHAPTER 2.

TUMOR BABY

"I'm going to inject you here in your arm where the fat is," she said.

"But there's no fat there," I deadpanned. "That's all Grade A muscle."

She frowned. "Here, in your arm, is fat."

"No," I said incredulously, "that's all muscle, from my bodybuilding days. You'll probably break the tip of your syringe."

"No, everyone has fat here," this time pointing to her own bony tricep. "It's the best place for the injection."

Earlier in pre-op that Monday morning, after removing every article of my clothes, even my wedding band, and putting on a gown decorated with Pink Floyd–meets–Dress Barn geometric designs, she had told me that her name, Chau, meant "pearls," which I found ironic, considering how I was throwing them at her to no affect or appreciation.

"Hi, my name is Chau," she'd said. "Is there anything I can get you?"

"Yeah, you don't happen to have a cure for cancer, do you?"

She paused as if she were running down the cafeteria's menu in her mind.

"No."

"I guess I'm fine then."

———————

My friends Dennis and Jeff had prayed over me that morning in the waiting room. Ali had already come back, and we'd cried and hugged and kissed and said the sorts of things that husbands and wives say to each other when they're scared shitless over what will follow when—not if—the other shoe drops. Those final moments with Ali revealed to me just how afraid I felt, not so much for me but for Ali and my boys. Gabriel and X had gone to school that morning knowing only that Daddy was having surgery to fix, as my son X put it, "the vaginate in his intestine."

We hadn't spoken the C-word in front of them.

Before the surgical team wheeled me back to the operating room, my friends Jeff and Dennis sat with me and prayed. Afterward, they let my mom come back to say good-bye, too. The team of surgical nurses waited by the curtain, wearing tan scrubs and plastic butcher's visors in front of their faces.

Exactly how much of my blood are you expecting to spray around the room?

They waited while my mom kissed me on the cheek and whispered into my ear, "I wish this were all happening to me and not you."

"Me too," I replied and waited a beat or two before smiling.

I turned to Chau, who was unplugging my IV from the wall, and said, "Chau, my mom's a nurse, and, well, it's sort of a family tradition—if it's OK with you, she'd like to be the one to put my catheter in."

"But she's not washed up," Chau replied.

By the grace of God, they put me under before they inserted the catheter, so I remain blissfully ignorant of whatever humiliating medieval torture such a procedure requires. I smiled broadly as I drifted off to sleep. I could've sworn I heard one of the surgical staff say aloud, "We're definitely going to need a bigger tube for the catheter."

Some dreams, I told myself with my last lucid thought, do come true.

Some nightmares do, too.

LARRY THE INVAGINATOR

The surgeon had told us on Friday she hoped to do the procedure laparoscopically. When I woke up on Monday evening, feeling like someone had gone at my gut with an electric Thanksgiving knife and a battery acid chaser, I suspected it had been a bigger surgery. In fact, they removed about three inches of my intestine to correct the inversion. They also removed from my small intestine a ten-by-ten-inch tumor baby, whom I've since taken affectionately to calling Larry.

Larry the Invaginator.

Ten by ten inches—it was about the size of a Stephen King novel. When its girth sank in with me, I immediately informed my mom that I could now understand what women go through in childbirth, which, I added, should make me even more appealing to the ladies (if such a feat is even possible). I took it as a positive sign that she managed to roll her eyes at me.

However, a ten-by-ten-inch tumor baby, unlike a real baby, is not an occasion for cigars and balloons.

The pathologist took initial slides of the tumor immediately after surgery. That evening, my brand-new oncologist, Dr. D—, told Ali and me that, even without the exact biopsy results, he knew I had a cancer that fell somewhere among five rare lymphomas.

We took the news about as badly as you'd imagine.

I'd gone to the doctor the previous week still thinking I had a gallstone or an ulcer, something not much more serious than a hairy mole. Forever I'd joked about how my body is a source of pride in me and arousal in women. The idea that my body was now trying to kill me was a complete shock to us.

Dr. D—'s caution that if I did nothing at all, I'd swiftly be dead was an even bigger shock.

We cried.

A lot.

I offered profuse and pathetic apologies for all the ways I'd been a crappy husband, all of which stemmed from that most common of betrayals: I assumed we had all the time in the world.

Luckily for me, it fell to Ali to go home and tell our boys, Gabriel and X, nine and twelve respectively, that *Daddy has cancer, which is what was making his tummy sick,* that *he's still sick,* and that *the doctors are going to work to make him better, but it's going to take a long time, and he'll be sicker in the meantime.* When Ali left me, I prayed Gabriel wouldn't recall how, in the middle of the year, his kindergarten teacher had died of cancer.

I wasn't there to see their reactions when Ali ushered them into this bad dream, but seeing the look of fear in Gabriel's eyes the next evening as he eyed the stomach tube coiling out of my nose, I could guess. He shut his eyes and shook his head *no* when I asked if he wanted to see where they'd operated on my tummy. After he left, I shut my eyes and shook my head *no* just like him.

Dr. D— returned to my hospital room the following evening. Pulling a chair up to my bed, he told us the results of my tumor's pathology. "You have mantle cell lymphoma," he told me straight up and then went on to explain how it's a rare, non-Hodgkin's form of B cell lymphoma.

Typically, he said—doctors are always using the word *typically*—mantle cell is only diagnosed in elderly men. I like to think I'm unique in all things, and it turns out I am in the case of diseases.

"It's spread through the GI system and bone marrow," he continued, pushing his wire-rimmed glasses back up his nose above his beard line. "Hence the tumor in your intestine."

Wisely, he directed the science to Ali.

It might've been the painkillers, but I hadn't fully processed his diagnosis, not until he used the word *aggressive* for the first time—as in "aggressive cancer."

"Because it's such an aggressive cancer," he made sure I was looking at him even as he spoke to Ali, "we'll have to fight it aggressively."

"You didn't say," I had to cough to find my voice, which my sore belly said was a bad decision, "what stage it is."

"Mantle cell isn't really staged in the same way as other cancers," he said, "because it never presents itself until it's already at what would be considered a stage 4 or 5 level of involvement."

"So I have stage 4-slash-5 cancer?" I asked.

"Think of it as *stage serious*," he answered.

Then he turned to my mom, a nurse, to describe the four two-part phases of aggressive chemotherapy, called R-HyperCVAD. Each phase, he explained, would last approximately four to eight weeks. At the end of the four-phase treatment, I would likely need to undergo bone marrow transplants as well.

He would order another CT scan, he said, this time of my entire body. "But based on the size of your tumor, I'm positive the lymphoma has spread throughout your body," he told me. "I know you're in pain from the surgery and don't want to hear this, but there is some urgency about this."

Urgency sounds worse than aggressive, I thought as Dr. D— told us that, after I recovered for a few days from my surgery, I would need to return to the hospital the following Friday to begin my initial chemotherapy treatment.

"We really can't wait any longer."

Just like that, I'd gone from thinking I would miss a few days from work to not knowing when I'd return. Or, I couldn't help but wonder, *if* I would ever return.

Still fuzzy from the painkillers, I wrote my congregation a note from my hospital bed, which, after breaking the C-word to them, I ended thus:

Like Bilbo Baggins, I have to go away for a while now.

I hope you continue to be around for us, though. I'm not normally given to sappy, sentimental nonsense, but I can't tell you how fortunate we feel to be going through this in a community we've come to know so well. Already so many of you have been key to getting us through the dark nights we've had. We're going to need you, and we're not the type to ask, so please don't wait for us to ask.

It might not surprise you, but my biggest fear—the thing that wakes me up in the middle of the night with panic attacks—has been about my boys. I don't want to put them through this, and I certainly don't want them to lose me or the family they know. You can help on their end, too. When you see them, please don't ask about me or my cancer. Please just treat them like normal kids, because a normal life for them is my biggest goal in all of this.

I miss you all. I really do, and I wish I could be there today to say all this to you. And don't sweat the God thing, people. Please.

I never believed before that God does mean-ass shit like this to people, so I'm not hung up on God doing it to me. I don't believe there's any mysterious "reason" other than the chromosomal one that cancer—however rare—is happening to me, and I don't believe there's a bigger plan behind all of this other than the same plan God has for all of us: to love and live like Jesus. I've just got to figure out how to do that given my new circumstances.

The coming months would test whether or not I'd still preach those lines about God, but then I closed the letter with this stoic command: "Finally, don't pity me."

Such bravado later made me cringe. I hadn't yet realized just how pitiable I would soon feel.

————————

Humiliated is more like it. Nor had I realized that *I* would be first one to pity me.

While the anesthesiologist had kept me mercifully ignorant of what installing the catheter entailed, removal of the catheter was a different story. In the days immediately after my intestinal surgery, I felt like my spleen would fall out through my sutured belly button if I as much as farted. But somehow I hurt more "down there."

You know where.

I'm sure it was psychosomatic, my mind attributing greater pain to that part of me that I, as a member of the male species, assign greater biological and spiritual significance. Sometime in the thick, languid days after surgery, a nurse technician named Jacqueline entered my room with an entourage of three and announced that she was there to remove my catheter.

"Aren't you going to, like, put me to sleep first?" I asked, feeling suddenly lucid. "Or anesthetize me?"

She waved her hand at me and smiled as if I were a rascally kindergartener. "Don't be a baby. You won't feel a thing."

"Won't feel a thing? You're going to pull a however-long tube out of my Magic Johnson. How is it *not* going to hurt?"

"With the meds you're on?" She frowned skeptically. "Tell me, can you feel anything down there now?"

"Yes," I lied.

She crossed her arms, casting a glance at the three women behind her. "Really? So can you feel that you're peeing right now as we speak?"

"I am?" I asked, pulling up the covers for a peek.

"Honey, you're telling me you just had a ten-by-ten-inch tumor taken out of your intestine, and you're worried about your *penis*?"

"Yes," I said flatly, thinking how the self-evidence of such a distinction should be just that, self-evident. "My intestines don't govern 97 percent of my waking and sleeping thoughts," I said.

She sighed like whatshername on *The View* and snapped

on a pair of gloves. Nodding her head to the Greek chorus behind her, she said, "They're interns. Do you mind if they watch and assist me?" Obviously "no" was the right answer, but considering how I was lassoed to the bed by ridiculous-looking compression socks, could barely move from the chainsawed gash in my gut, and was tethered to the wall behind me by the stomach tube extruding from my left nostril, I figured it was better at least to act as if I were in control.

"Sure," I said. "Maybe you should lower the lights and put some music on first."

All four of them rolled their eyes.

The narrator in one of John Irving's novels observes that the most emasculating position for any man is with his T-shirt on and nothing else. I used to think that sounded exactly right—that is, until Jacqueline pulled down my blankets and sheets to my ankles and then pulled my gown up past my weeping incision and swollen belly to around my nipples.

The rather zealous pre-op shave job they'd done on me, combined with the preschool-colored socks with rubber tread on my feet, somehow made me look even more pathetic.

One of Jacqueline's students took my lifeless unit in one latexed hand and the catheter tube in the other. Then Jacqueline came around behind her and put her hands on top of the intern's so as to demonstrate the proper positioning and technique, as though we were on a putting green somewhere and Jacqueline was the club pro using not a putter or a five iron for her lesson but my baloney pony.

"What do you for a living?" Jacqueline asked me while her intern found the right spots.

"Uh, I'm a . . . uh . . . a minister," I said.

"Praise Jesus!" nurse Jacqueline exclaimed with a sincerity that seemed to match her volume. And just then, she started to slowly pull what felt somewhere inside me like a thirty-foot length of raggedy twenty-pound saltwater fishing line from my bait and tackle.

Now, I'd be lying if I claimed that the image of four women gathered around my naked body praising Jesus as they beheld my manhood was a scene that had never once played in the cinema of my teenage mind, but as far as fantasies go, this wasn't it. When you're a guy, the last thing you want is for your piece to be held in a woman's hand as limp and lifeless as roadkill. And you definitely don't fantasize that said woman will wear an absolutely vacant expression on her face.

As she neared the catheter's end, Jacqueline warned me, "You'll probably go pee-pee on yourself when this comes all the way out."

Seriously, she said "pee-pee."

As if my multiple injuries needed the extra insult, I promptly did precisely that. Pee-peed all over myself, and somehow *pee-pee* seemed exactly the right word for how silly and emasculated I felt. Right then, I became the first person to violate my stiff-lipped command to my congregation.

Another of her interns tossed me an adult-size baby wipe.

"You can clean yourself off," she said in a way that made feel like I was supposed to get up and leave money on the IV stand. Actually, no. That's bullshit.

No, it just made me feel *humiliated.*

Such were the hours and days after catheter day.

It had been less than a week since the night Dr. P—

called and asked me if I was sitting down. A few days, however, was plenty of time for me to learn that humiliation is one of the ways stage-serious cancer manifests itself:

- Needing help to pee into the plastic jug because you don't have the ab muscles to do even that for yourself

- Needing help to change your gown at three o'clock in the morning because—fun fact—night sweats are one of the symptoms of the cancer that's now coursing through your blood

- Needing the surgical resident to pretend she doesn't notice the crack in your voice and the tears welling up around your eyes as she asks how you're doing

As surely as a cold begets a runny nose, this cancer had brought humiliation into a life where ironic pretense and playing it cool had been the norm. For example, the third or fourth night in the hospital, the nurse, who was about to check my vital signs in the middle of the night, was standing there in the dark just as I woke up suddenly, crying and breathless from the first of what would become regular panic attacks. She wiped the sweat from my forehead, tucked me in, and shushing me, said, "It's going to be all right, sweetie."

Like I was a child.

A pitiable child.

In those first few days, I heard from lots of people, and many of them asked me what it's like, having this giant steaming pile of crap land in the middle of my life. And honestly, the first word that came to mind was *humiliating.*

Susan Sontag, who died of cancer herself, wrote, "It

is not suffering as such that is most deeply feared but suffering that degrades."

It was the beginning of Lent, the season when Christians imitate Jesus' journey to the cross, so perhaps the question would've struck me even if I hadn't gotten sick, but with cancer, the question certainly felt more relevant.

Here's the question:

- Does Christ participate in our suffering and humiliation?
- Or do we participate in Christ's suffering and humiliation?

If the answer is the former, then that means there is no permutation of our humanity in which Christ has not been made present. Whatever we go through, the theological line continues, we can go through it knowing our suffering is not unknown to God. God, like Bill Clinton, feels our pain.

There's nothing wrong with that answer, I suppose. But suddenly, I found good news in the latter. We participate in Christ's suffering and humiliation by our own. Just like the bumper sticker, a lot of people treat Jesus as though he's the answer to our problems and questions: How can I be saved? Why do bad things happen to good people? How can I find prosperity?

But if we participate in Christ's humiliation and suffering through our own, then that means Jesus isn't an answer to our problems and questions. Rather, Jesus gives a means of living amidst life's problems and questions.

Can you feel the distinction? Ever since that night I had to swallow my pride and ask the nurse to help change me, I could feel the distinction. Feeling humiliated on an almost hourly basis, I didn't need or want a God who could feel my humiliation, who shared my pain. I needed, desperately wanted, a God whose own life can show me a way to live in and through it.

'TIL DEATH DO US PART

Then again, maybe the reason I didn't need a God who shared my pain was that I already had Ali, sharing it with me.

Having been pastor for fifteen years, I've worked with I don't know how many couples, and one of the points I've always impressed upon those about to be married is what I tell them is "Jason's rule." It goes like this: You never really know the person you're marrying until after you've been married to the person you're marrying.

Jason's rule is just a shamelessly cribbed version of Hauerwas's rule, named after the theologian Stanley Hauerwas. Whether you have a terrific relationship or a terrible one, I always tell couples before their wedding and often repeat in my wedding sermon for them, Jason's rule always holds true. "I don't care if you've already lived with the person you're marrying or if you've filled out a hundred eHarmony compatibility questions; Jason's rule always prove true."

I've preached several dozen wedding homilies. "Marriage," I tell the couples, stealing from Hauerwas again, "names the process in which you discover who the stranger is that you've married (as well as who the stranger is that you call you)." That's why I always warn them before they ever promise anything about sickness and health or riches and poverty or death parting them, "Marriage isn't just a beautiful leap of faith, it's a rough-

and-tumble process, too. It's why even the best marriages aren't easy or painless."

But cancer's funny.

While I still think Jason's rule is a nugget of ostensible wisdom worth doling out to couples, cancer caused me to reconsider it. Contrary to my own premarital dictate, cancer caused me to realize that I knew all along exactly who I was marrying.

The rule still holds true in the sense that Ali never foresaw that when I vowed, "And with all that I am," mantle cell lymphoma was in there, too. But even though I didn't know back then that my chromosomes would one day foment a mutiny within my marrow, I *did* know—yes, I absolutely did—that Ali is the type of person who would gently shush me and smooth my sweat-matted hair when a panic attack roused me awake.

Before she ever promised to love and comfort me in sickness, I knew that she would change my soiled gown and hospital sheets in the middle of the night. Being young and stupid, I had no notion such a day would come, but I still knew she was the type of woman who would never reconsider the fairness of the forsaking-all-others promise while she knocked softly on the door of the hospital bathroom to ask if I was all right, as I struggled with my first post-op poo.

My premarital advice aside, I knew when I said "I do," she would do all of this and more. One of the things you learn in ministry—what the average cancer patient (or doctor even) might not know—is the degree to which stage-serious cancer can wreak havoc on a marriage. That's why it's so grave—as in important—that I knew before either us pledged anything about "for better, for worse" that Ali was the sort of person for whom this would never be just my cancer. Ali is an *our* kind of woman, and as soon as I awoke from surgery, it became our disease.

Actually, Dr. D— wasn't the first one to deliver my diagnosis to me. Ali did.

Ali had to be the one to put on a brave face and break the news to me when I first opened my eyes out of surgery: "It was a bigger surgery than they thought, honey. They removed a pretty large tumor. It's lymphoma. We're waiting to find out what kind."

Of course, I was too narced up to remember her telling me any of it, but my mom was there, and later she told me how Ali did a good job with the hard telling.

I didn't need a God who shared my pain, because it was *our* cancer, Ali's and mine.

I never knew we'd be in this position, just over a dime into our marriage, but when I said, "I do," I just knew, if only intuitively, what Ali would do. Without meaning to sound creepy or more prescient than I am, it's one of the reasons I married her. It only took a few days of us having cancer to make me suspect I'd been wrong in all that pastoral advice. Now that we had cancer, I realized I knew exactly who Ali was all along. And that Ali was ready to help me die.

———————

There's a scene in John's Gospel where Jesus kneels down, dons the posture of a servant, and washes his friends' feet. Peter and the others initially resist; preachers almost always interpret their reluctance in terms of exaltation and humiliation. Peter and the others, it's assumed, don't want a king like Jesus deigning to wash their nasty feet. Therefore discipleship, the sermons always go, entails stooping down, rolling up our sleeves, swallowing our pride, and serving like Christ.

Cancer's funny. It made that story refreshingly unfamiliar to me. For example, I noticed how, in the story, what Peter resists isn't what Jesus does—acting beneath his station and washing their feet. No, Peter resists what Jesus says—that this foot washing is a sharing in Jesus' death.

It's not that Peter doesn't want Jesus to wash his feet.

It's that Peter doesn't want to die.

No doubt it owed to the many times Ali washed the panicked sweat from my forehead, but after we received the news we'd both dreaded, worse than we'd even feared, I thought a lot about another washing we do in the church, baptism. Specifically, I thought about how in the church we say with water and oil that the baptized are baptized into Christ's death.

Christians mean that literally if obliquely.

The manner in which we carry our own crosses, confront adversity, and, say, deal with stage-serious disease are ways we live into our baptisms, sharing—hopefully later rather than sooner—in Christ's death.

I've always enjoyed pointing out to would-be newlyweds how the wedding liturgy comes after the baptism liturgy. The latter depends upon the former for its intelligibility. Marriage—with its impossibly huge promises of constancy, come what may until death tears us asunder—is but a way we live into and live out our baptisms. I can't tell you how many would-be newlyweds have told me they want to get married because they've found the person with whom they want to share their life.

Truly, if the worship book is any clue, we should be

searching for a rarer kind of person—someone with whom we can die. No, even rarer still: someone who can help us die in a manner worthy of our baptism.

But hopefully, as Ali kept telling me, that moment comes later rather than soon. When you learn you have cancer, you realize Neil Young had it all wrong. Only a fool would fail to realize it's much better to fade away into old age.

ANOTHER ONE BITES THE DUST

My last night in the hospital, Ali climbed into my hospital bed with me and gently lay down beside me, resting her head on the nasty bile tube running from my gut out my nose.

The next day, before I left the hospital, per my oncologist's orders, I had a dual-lumen port installed in my chest, just opposite my heart. It was a device—an accessory if you will—into which the poison would flow when I returned in a week for my first bout of chemotherapy.

An orderly named Nathaniel wheeled me down from my room to a unit whose name I missed in the wincing, DUI-like jingle-jangle that was Nathaniel hitting every bump, corner, laundry bin, and stray wheelchair along the way.

In his defense, he was distracted.

Nathaniel was Ethiopian, which I could tell from his complexion and his accent. He was, he told me freely and for no apparent reason, an Orthodox Christian, which led to my ill-advised confession to being a man of the cloth. As soon as Nathaniel found out I was a "priest" (which happened just as we passed my nurse's station), he ceased looking at the route ahead of the $35,000 bed to which I was chained by way of compression socks and IV needle, and instead he zeroed his attention on my "sense of peace here in the hospital."

"It must be wonderful," he rhapsodized. "Feeling the Holy Spirit overshadow you."

Is this guy serious? Or is it the morphine?

But what I said was, "I don't know, Nathaniel. The Holy Spirit overshadowed Mary, and she wound up an unwed teenage mother. I'm not so sure I need any overshadowing on top of the scary stage-serious cancer in my marrow."

But Nathaniel wasn't listening to me. At all. He was too excited about having a genuine Christian talisman in his presence, albeit one—according to the nurses—with strong vital signs and alive for at least a little while longer.

"With the Holy Spirit, I imagine you feel no pain, no pain at all," Nathaniel said beatifically, just as he bumped the side of my bed against the elevator door, sending what felt like a 9.0 fart engulfed in flames through my recently incised insides.

Once delivered to my pre-op bay, I waited while several nurses stopped by my bed to reassure me how I would "experience no pain" while they sank what looked like a diaphragm with purple spermatozoa into my chest and attached it my jugular.

"You're not going to knock me out?" I asked in disbelief.

"We'll administer a mild sedative. You won't feel a thing."

"Really? How many of them do you have installed in your chest?" I asked.

Huffing at the pain-in-the-ass impossibility that was patient 5421, she walked away, only to return a few minutes later to explain how if my chest port ever got infected, then it would (a) be excruciatingly painful, (b) "compromise my treatment," and (c) "quite possibly kill" immune-deficient me.

"Kick ass," I said, like Maverick about to take off.

They wheeled me into a room that had a dank *12 Monkeys* feel to it, where the nurse pitilessly instructed me to climb onto the operating table, which in my sutured, doped-up state was like asking John Goodman to scale a pommel horse.

Holding my stitched and stapled bowels with my left hand and trying to cover my bare behind with my right, I attempted a "maneuver" that felt (and probably looked) like a full-body dry heave. I wound up on my face, leaning over my splayed out knees, with my hairy, sponge-bathed butt sticking up in the air. Seeing my futility, they picked me up and moved me the way lifeguarding students handle accident dummies.

They laid me out on the table, wrapped a sort of inflatable mattress around my circumference, and positioned my head across my left shoulder—so I couldn't be a witness to the carnage to come, I suspected. Informing me they'd just administered a mild sedative, someone (who I couldn't see but who smelled of Axe body spray) took to shaving my chest.

"Sigh," I sighed.

I'd already had one shave job that week.

"Say," I said, "If I gave you fifty dollars cash, would you just go ahead and give me a full body wax?"

"Not during working hours," Axe Body Spray replied creepily. When he finished his hasty man-scaping, a bracing sensation struck me.

"Is that . . . rubbing alcohol?" I asked, feeling the liquid ignite all over me—especially around my nipples—before dripping down my sides.

"Yes," he said.

"Lovely," I said. "For a second there, I forgot about the bone-crunching pain in my gut."

Like I said, I'd already gotten one half-assed shave job before my intestinal surgery, and now, thanks to Axe Body Spray, from my twig and berries to my Adam's apple, the only hair on my upper body resided on that shoulder mole.

And my hands.

Seriously, my top half now looked like the love child of Justin Bieber and Samwise Gamgee. Actually, given my weight loss, I looked more like the bastard child produced by a Keira Knightley affair with a short-order cook from a Greek diner.

Like I said, lovely. (Now you know why I know about merkins.)

As the drowsiness set on me, the nurse asked, "What kind of music do you like?"

"Oh, just about anything," I lied to avoid conversation.

"Bluegrass?" she asked.

"Actually, yeah, I like bluegrass a lot," I responded.

"Hmm, not me," she said before turning it to what I could tell was one of those soft-pop stations that purport to play "the best songs from the '80s." Sure enough, Tears for Fears were just finishing up wanting to rule the world when the Belinda Carlisle song "Heaven on Earth" kicked on. Just as I was going lights-out to the world, I considered that if Belinda's right, if heaven is a place on earth, then (in addition to Cleveland and Walt Disney World), heaven is anywhere but here. Near me.

I woke up without realizing I'd been asleep. "Everything OK?" I asked, not even sure if they'd begun.

"Sure," the nurse said. "You didn't move at all, except when you bounced your hips a little to 'Raspberry Beret.'"

I blinked my eyes awake and felt the dull ache in my baby-bottom chest, just opposite my heart. I turned my head and saw the purple wires with input heads on the end dangling down my torso.

When I showed the chest port to my boys later that evening, they both immediately compared it to Tony Stark's arc light reactor. It's not a bad analogy. The arc reactor not only powers Iron Man's suit but also keeps Tony's body from slowly poisoning itself.

The chest port also resembled auxiliary audio cables coming out of my breast. The effect was to make me look like a piece of stereo equipment, as though if you stuck an antenna up my bum and plugged me into a speaker, I could play *All Things Considered* for you.

Or, I kept thinking, *music.* As I waited to be discharged that afternoon, I wondered, *If you plugged me into a car stereo or a surround sound system, what music would MP3 me play? What soundtrack for the movie* Jason Has Cancer *is recorded there just across from my heart?* I imagine the cuts from my prediagnosis days would include something like R.E.M.'s "Shiny Happy People" or maybe something from Van Morrison's *Astral Weeks* and Miles's *Birth of the Cool* album. When I expressed my first fart after surgery, which was the sign they'd put Humpty's insides back together again, I probably would've played "I'm So Excited." And when I dropped my first post-op deuce, I would've blasted Handel's Hallelujah Chorus, or maybe Elton's "Rocket Man."

Or, since we're talking crap, I thought, *anything by Coldplay.*

That last night, when Ali climbed into the hospital bed with me, damning my leaky bile tube and lying right on top of it, and she wiped the night sweat off of me and held me until the nurse made her get out, I would have belted out Phil Collins's power ballad "Against All Odds." Over and over.

I just prayed I didn't come with a hidden bonus track, one that wasn't listed when you bought the album but had been there the whole time nonetheless and couldn't be deleted: Queen's "Another One Bites the Dust."

THE CHRISTIAN FEAR OF FEAR

The funny thing about fear when you're a Christian (especially a pastor) is how other Christians treat fear like it's anathema. Verboten. More cancerous than cancer, like it's a tumor that threatens the body of Christ.

To be afraid, to pay attention to the prognosis, to weigh the odds and fear where you'll end—all of it, many unwittingly imply, is the opposite of faith, according to many Christians. After all, if you trust God, then you shouldn't fear what tomorrow will bring.

- Let go and let God.

- Give it over to the Lord.

- Trust Jesus.

- Everything happens for a reason.

- He never gives you more than you can handle.

- Have faith that all will be well, and all will be well, and all manner of things will be well.

- Whatever happens, he has a plan.

- Have faith, not fear.

I recoiled at the many well-meaning clichés I heard in that first week, but I suppose Christians come by it honestly, this fear-versus-faith way of thinking. "Don't be afraid" is perhaps the most common refrain in the testaments. God, the angel Gabriel, and Jesus himself are constantly telling people not to fear.

One of those first nights in the hospital, when I couldn't sleep and was flipping channels on the TV, a bouffant preacher hawking a Bible study curriculum on the Trinity Broadcasting Network reminded me how the New Testament letter from John says that fear is the opposite of faith and how perfect love (for the Lord) casts out all fear. From where I sat, that sounded like horse shit, even if it is in the Bible. *And*, I thought, *I'm not even sure it's true.*

Sure, it's true if what John means is that love—as in Love, as in Jesus—casts out all fear. It's true if what John's really after is that faith, as in Jesus' faith, is the opposite of our fear. Maybe it's even true if what John has in mind is causation: that is, provoking faith and love in someone is the opposite of provoking fear in someone.

Sure.

But otherwise, the notion, hawked by that TV preacher and so many other well-meaning Christians, that the presence of fear equals the absence of love felt like total rubbish. If there's one thing stage-serious cancer does, it's inject an ample dose of clarity into your life.

And here's what my dosage revealed: I was afraid because I love.

I wasn't especially afraid for myself, for what the treatment or the cancer would do to me. I wasn't afraid of the pain or discomfort. I figured that if I could live for a month with a ten-by-ten-inch tumor obstructing my poop chute, I could handle chemo and bone marrow transplants.

I was not afraid for me.

I was afraid because I loved.

I feared what cancer would do to my boys, to their happiness and joy and innocence and faith.

While we're on the subject of faith, doing cancer as a Christian can be hard enough for many folks; doing cancer as a public, professional Christian was something I was only beginning to sort out. It felt like someone had thrown me a gown and I was still trying to find the arms. Not only was my faith expected to be a resource for me while cancer tried to kill me, it was expected that my faith, in its death match versus cancer, would be a resource for others, too. After just three exhausting days, I could honestly say I didn't know if I could do it—fight cancer in a fishbowl.

And I feared what cancer would do to my congregation's faith when they saw one of their pastors handed a huge crap-flavored lollipop. Speaking of church, I was afraid of the stress this placed on my colleagues, who got left holding the bag with literally a day's notice. I was afraid that if and when I returned to work, it would be as a shell of my former self.

I feared the burden and grief cancer would bring my friends and family; I actually visualized seeing it in their eyes. I feared the toll my cancer would take on my wife. I feared losing not our marriage or our family but the life—the freaking perfect life—we had built and enjoyed with our kids. It's impossible to exaggerate how I also feared the practicalities like what cancer would cost us, and therefore what it would cost us in terms of the dreams and goals we'd previously harbored.

I was riddled with fear during that first week in the hospital, and for Saint John or a hair-sprayed TV preacher or a well-meaning well-wisher to suggest it meant I lacked faith or love seemed to me to be completely tone-deaf. If I didn't have so much and so many I loved, I wouldn't have given a damn, and I really could face cancer with a brave-face stoicism. But because I did love, much and many, there was no way around it. I was afraid. If that somehow put me at odds with Jesus, I figured we'd have to sort it out when I met him later.

"God," I prayed, "I want it to be later."

If you plugged MP3 me into a surround sound, you know what track you wouldn't have heard playing from somewhere just west of my heart? Neil Young's "Hey Hey, My My." You'd never hear it because of that line from the chorus, where Neil sings, "It's better to burn out / Than to fade away. . . ."

Ali wouldn't have it. She was determined we'd grow old and gray and fade away together. In the meantime, I chose to ignore the Johns and the TV preachers and trust that if the people in my life were worth Jesus redeeming, then they were worth my fears, too.

CHAPTER 3.

CHEMO SISSY

When Dr. D— first broke the news to me, I assumed cancer was a bad thing. I assumed that just because I had a rare, incurable, quite possibly terminal lymphoma that would require searing treatment and scads of cash, a disease that would take a harrowing emotional toll on me and mine while—best-case scenario—reducing me to a gaunt, hairless, infertile ("probably *not*"), impotent shadow of my former healthy, virile self, that it was all downside.

As it turns out, I discovered in the week after my surgery, cancer is not without its uses. Cancer, I learned in the days before I started chemo, is like having an ace in the hole you can play whenever it suits you without ever having to leave the card on the table. For example, driving to my oncologist's office the morning before my chemo began, my wife and I found ourselves running late.

"Just speed," I said calmly from the passenger seat. "You'll make up the time."

"On this road?" she replied in a voice implying I had prophylactic chemo brain. "There are speed traps everywhere. We'll get pulled over for sure."

"Maybe," I accepted. "But then all you have to say is, 'I'm sorry, officer, we're late for my husband's appointment with his oncologist. He has [dab the eye] . . . cancer.' Even the most tight-sphinctered cop wouldn't give you a ticket."

The cancer-house-always-wins odds washed over her. She glanced at me, her eyes glinting like Steve McQueen's to Ali MacGraw in *The Getaway*.

"Punch it, baby," I said. "When life hands you a belly full of tumorous lemons, then make lemonade."

During the week I spent at home post-op/pre-chemo, one afternoon a pimpled idealist with a five-dollar T-shirt and a plastic lanyard came knocking at my front door, canvassing for some urgent political cause. Having pimped out my principles for such work myself back in college, I'm normally an easy mark for a sympathetic signature and a harmless chunk of change. This time, though, I didn't even have to resort to my typical "I was just making dinner" excusing salvo. Nope. Channeling my genuine and recent sense of bewilderment, I muttered, "I'm sorry. . . . I just found out. . . . I have cancer. . . ."

When I said it—and truthfully, I don't even know why I said it (I'm an ass might be one obvious answer)—I wasn't expecting it to slink me free of her utopian overtures.

But sure enough, no sooner had the C-word left my lips than she was forcibly removing her clipboard from my hands as though its germs might infect neutropenic me. Grabbing her ballpoint pen and boldfaced brochure back from me, she affected a preschool teacher's countenance and said, "You don't need to worry about this right now, and you *certainly* don't need to be giving away money." For a second, I thought she was going to hug me. She looked like she was going to cry, and more importantly, I did not look fifty dollars lighter for it.

See, I thought to myself as I closed the door behind her. *Who said cancer is a bad thing?*

Just the day before, my cellphone had interrupted me while I'd been changing the dressing on my stomach incision. It was someone from the car dealership, trying to persuade me with the slick logic of a payday loan to save money by trading in my nearly paid-for car for a new completely unpaid-for one. I'd met this salesperson several times before, and each time, he left me feeling as if I needed a shower. If I'd been splurting blood from the jugular such that it was spraying Cormac McCarthy–style all over the ceiling, I would've bet a down payment that he'd still pressure me into an extended warranty before applying pressure to my sputtering wound.

But I was wrong. "I'm sorry," I said a few seconds into his cellphone shtick. "I actually just got discharged from the hospital. Turns out I've got . . . cancer."

The conversation was over as quickly as it had begun. And bonus, he sent me a sympathy card.

The C-word got me out of the change fees with an airline for a trip I had planned to take with my wife in the spring but now could not "because [deep, melancholy sigh] I have . . . cancer."

"Merci," I said to the customer service lady in Quebec City when she processed a full refund.

To those with the (hairless) balls to grab the tumor by the reins, cancer is like the cellular equivalent of that long Steadicam tracking shot in *Goodfellas*. Sure, like the mob, cancer puts your life at risk, but at least it makes you a made guy, opening doors with barely four syllables' worth of effort.

Even better, cancer can close down unwanted conversations faster than asking, "Would you mind if I talked to you about Jesus?"

Cancer's not all bad, I told myself. Of course, I tried convincing myself of this before I had even set a single foot in my oncologist's office.

THE WEIGHTING ROOM

My initial office visit had been scheduled for the day before my chemo was to begin. When I walked into the office, I instantly thought of that line inscribed onto the Statue of Liberty: "Give me your tired, your poor, your huddled masses yearning to breathe free." We can debate whether Lady Liberty's salutation has ever accurately reflected America's attitude toward the stranger; however, as a description of the insides of an oncologist's waiting room, it's a dead ringer. Previously accustomed only to the PG blandness of my general practitioner's office or my children's trippy, panda-themed pediatrician's office, I found myself wholly unprepared for what hit me:

- The sheer size of the oncologist's waiting room—It was so large, I half expected to hear a fuzzy intercom announcing bus departures from the other side of thick, yellowed Plexiglas.

- The sense of hopelessness that hung in the air—I was struck by how thick and tangible it was.

- The diversity embodied by that palpable despair—Sitting along the walls were couples the approximate age of Ali and me; old, white-haired geezers; folks in their fifties; healthy-looking women;

obese men; alienesque pale, balding, and rail-thin chemo patients; and kids.

Man, the effing kids. I counted seven of them. School-age kids during the school day. Instantly, they made me wonder if there were a simpler explanation than that God was playing hooky from creation. *Weighting* room seemed a better spelling for where I was, given the gravity I could feel in my feet as I soon as I stepped inside.

The wall scheme, as if avoiding false promises, was mauve. No color. No toys or play structures for the children. And in a medical-office first for me, there were no magazines. Not one. Their collective absence stood out like an indictment or a more bracing diagnosis than even the doctor could muster.

You're not getting away anywhere with the time you've got left, screamed the bare space where *Condé Nast Traveler* might've been. The bare space on the end table next to my chair taunted me: *Who are you kidding? You don't need 25 Sex Tips from* Cosmopolitan. *Those days are gone.*

Speaking of sex, this oncological consult just before I was to begin my aggressive (read: dire) chemo protocol was not the occasion on which I had expected to have a conversation about sex. Specifically, my swimmers. But sure enough, no sooner was I weighed and vital-signed than my oncologist knocked on the door, entered the exam room, and with the subtlety of someone who is either a lifelong bachelor or a non–English major, immediately began by asking me, "So, you two have children, yes?"

"Uh, yeah, we have two. Two boys."

"I see," he said. "And do you plan to have more?"

We looked blankly at each other. "I dunno. I mean we've talked about the possibility maybe, but. . . ."

"Because if you do want to have more children, you'll have to make a donation this morning before you start treatment."

"Uh, a donation?"

"Yes, a sperm donation," he said as though itemizing my taxes.

I don't know why, since I'd been married to Ali for almost fourteen years and we started dating when we were fifteen years old, but I still found this an intensely awkward conversation to be having in front of her—not to mention the nurse sitting at the computer. And as I'm wont to do in embarrassing situations, I resorted to deflective, juvenile humor, albeit based on a classic Woody Allen line from *Annie Hall*: "Look, Doc," I said. "I've got nothing against masturbation; it's sex with someone I love."

The nurse at the computer—the nurse who happened to be wearing a 14.5-inch bleeding-Christ crucifix around her neck—looked at me with disgust and at Ali with something like pity.

"Anyway, Doc," I said, "you should've brought this up before you let the surgeon cut a giant incision across my waist, because things are still as dormant down there as Omaha on a Saturday night, if you know what I mean."

Whether he did or didn't know what I meant, he didn't say, adding only this turd of a caveat: "Your protocol probably won't render you impotent, but it will leave you infertile."

"Probably?" I gulped.

I suppose sex and death have been inextricably linked since Eve's and Adam's fall from grace. I suppose it was ever thus; nonetheless, just as I wasn't expecting to begin my final oncological consult with talk of ejaculatory donations, the transition out of that subject was even more jarring.

There was another knock at the door, and my other oncologist entered the room. His first name was Ivan, and his last name ended in -*vich*. The closet approximation I can get to the rest of his surname is to say it leaves no consonant behind.

Dr. Ivan was tall and thin and Serbian, a scary representative of the land from which he hailed. His thin, round glasses looked party issue. His hair was mussed in the way of someone committed to the cause, and his accent was such that it was easy to picture him wearing a drab, olive uniform, smoking a hand-rolled cigarette, and standing behind one-way glass while a lieutenant conducted an "interrogation."

In short, he was everything a scared-shitless, cancer-stricken bastard like me could want in an oncologist on the front line.

Describing the next 150 days or so of my R-HyperCVAD regimen, Dr. Ivan opted for martial vocabulary and large Saint Crispin's Day–type hand gestures. My first drug, he said with a smack of his hands, "will obliterate the bulky tumors all over your body."

"The other drugs will *devastate the enemy cells* multiplying in the blood," he whispered as if it were a sneak attack on unsuspecting Kosovars. And then, rising off his stool, he promised the cumulative effect would be to "force my bone marrow into *complete submission*."

If Dr. Ivan seemed like the kind of medical professional you'd come across in the pages of an X-Men comic book, he merely stood in and continued a long line in the study of oncology. After all, the practice of chemotherapy itself owes its origins to the use of mustard gas in World War I. True story. Not only was mustard gas a nasty little way to debilitate your enemy, it was also discovered to be an effective suppressor of blood production. Skip ahead to WWII. After a German air raid on the Italian village of Bari, several hundred people were inadvertently exposed to mustard gas the Allies had been storing there to be used on the Germans. Oh, happy accident: the survivors were all found to have abnormally low white blood counts. Thus is the beginning of another chapter in the supposedly value-neutral discipline of medical science.

So I can't be accused of hyperbole when I say that the following day, I was a duly admitted patient at a medical hospital (modernity's last true cathedral), where doctors and nurses could legally assault me with German-derived chemical weapons.

The trench warfare history of chemo-"therapy" such as it is, I shouldn't have been surprised at how my first dosage went down. After pre-scans of my body and pre-hydrations and pre-medications, around 1:30 a.m. my nurse on the cancer ward started my first six-hour IV drip of Rituxan, a poison normally considered safe only for Mantle Cell Lymphoma (MCL) patients who are "young and fit."

"'Young and fit' minus the, you know, stage 4/5 cancer all over my body," I muttered to my mom, who was riding shotgun with me that first night.

Not knowing what to anticipate from the Rituxan, I lay there in bed that first night, clutching the sheets in the quiet. Nothing.

I was fine. I couldn't feel or notice a thing.

By 2 a.m., I was smiling in the dark. At myself. Thinking

to myself, *Paul Simon's got it all wrong. The darkness isn't silent; it's filled with sound of my awesomeness.*

"Who are these sissies," I wondered to mother, "who complained about how hard chemo is on the body?"

I'm like the Charles Bronson of chemo. I'm like Jules from the lymphoma outtakes of Pulp Fiction. *I'm a mushroom-cloud-laying mofo. I'm like the* Taken 1, 2, *and* 3 *Liam Neeson of chemo-"weaponry"; I have a very particular set of skills, and kicking cancer's ass is one of them.*

I seriously thought that to myself.

And then BAM. At 3 a.m., ninety minutes in, with no warning at all, I went from zero to sixty in one second flat. My whole body started to convulse, violently, head to toe, shaking my bed and every machine attached to it, splitting open my stomach incision and making my insides feel like they were now my outsides. It was like an epileptic seizure—but one that started not in my brain, but in this dry-ice cold deep down inside my bone marrow.

It was 3 a.m., chemo battle number one, and what did the Charles Bronson of cancer do?

That's right, he shouted—not really shouted, because the words wouldn't really come out of his quaking mouth—gurgled for his mommy, who was snoring on the pullout bed in his room. My mom fetched the nurse, who upon entering, blithely responded with "Oh, yes, that's one of the reactions to the Rituxan," as she started layering a dozen warmed blankets on me to zero effect.

Reaction? Hives from bad Cabernet is a reaction. A rash from a bug bite is a reaction.

Except actually, I wasn't thinking. At all. I couldn't think past the pain the convulsions had erupted all over me. I couldn't have made heads or tails of a *Two and a Half*

Men episode or a Sarah Palin speech, so bone-wracking was the pain. It was blinding, consuming. A first for me.

It lasted about an hour.

And if you had offered me in any of those sixty minutes anything to make it stop, to take it away, to turn back time—to any of my worst precancer moments—then, damn the torpedoes, I would've taken you up on it.

No.

That's not true.

I love my life. I cherish my wife. And I'm gunning to see my little guys grow up.

I would've stuck it out for them, no matter what you offered me.

But, brass tacks confession time: If you told me then the next 150 days would be exactly like that hour and if you could promise me to make it all go away, then I wouldn't say yes because of the reasons immediately cited above. I don't think, but I'd be tempted. And that means I could have said say yes.

ASHES TO ASHES

A couple of days before I started chemo, my church marked the beginning of Lent by marking their foreheads with ashen crosses, recalling their mortality with the words "From dust you came, and to dust you shall return," and reading the story of Jesus' temptation in the wilderness.

Whenever we picture Jesus tempted by the devil in the wilderness, we usually imagine it in unsubtle comic book lines and hues, with a bad guy readily identifiable as "Satan" and three temptations to which Jesus readily gives the correct answers as though he's been raised by a Galilean Tiger Mom.

The evangelists tell the story with such Hollywood haste that they effectively turn Jesus of Nazareth into a spiritual prodigy who doesn't scratch his head over the best way forward. But not only is such convictional clarity not temptation, it dilutes Jesus into someone less than fully human. It makes Jesus not as human as you or me. I know the Gospels say Jesus was tempted by the devil in the desert, and I believe it. I just think those temptations came to Jesus in exactly the same sorts of unseen, uncertain, ambiguous—human—ways they come to us.

I mean, it's a no-brainer if you're posed questions by a guy with horns and a pitchfork. The right answers are obvious; that's not temptation. Which is to say, I take it as an article of faith that it was a real, live possibility for Jesus to have answered otherwise when the tempter proffered his questions in the desert. Just take another look; the brevity of the stories aside, Jesus spends forty days tackling just three queries. That's a baker's dozen days per temptation. There's more to the story than the story.

We tend to think of faith as something unchanging and immovable, which we can turn to when times get tough or tempting. "He is our Rock," the praise song repeats ad nauseam. Faith is our North Star, our inner compass, our firm foundation.

But I don't think so, not since that first night of chemo.

If Jesus is at least as human as you or me, then one of the things Jesus takes on in the incarnation is the contingency of life—not knowing what will drop with the next shoe, what crappy news is a day away, or what will be the best way to deal with it. If Jesus is at least as human as you or me, then his humanity is shot through with the very uncertainty that so often makes our lives seem like a crapshoot. And that means faith isn't like a rock or a firm, immovable foundation. It means faith is as ever changing as everything else in our lives.

Faith entails change because it's faith that unfolds in the world God has given us. Faith requires change even, for faith depends upon the always-changing life in which it is lived. In the same way that love and marriage and children and a career change you—and thus your faith—so do pain and dread and fear and despair and temptation change you—and thus your faith.

What makes temptation in the face of faith real is the real possibility of losing the faith you had. The real possibility of failing at your faith or—here's what you discover is truly scary—finding that your faith fails you when you most need it.

If there's a silver lining there (and cancer has made me a seeker of silver linings), it's that "faith is strongest," as poet Christian Wiman posits, "where the possibility of doubt is greatest."

"One day down," I told my mom the next morning, "149 or so more to go."

I didn't add how that was nearly four times longer than Jesus was stuck in his own wilderness.

ETERNITY IS THE WRONG DAMN NUMBER

On the third day of my treatment, in the middle of the afternoon, a pious-eyed chaplaincy student from the seminary just down the road wandered into my room.

As I had designated my religion as "Christian" at patient registration, she had arrived to offer me, as she uncertainly and nervously put it, "pastoral care." I've been in her shoes before, making the hospital rounds and intruding upon patients who have difficulty hiding how they'd rather not have you there, so I tried to be on my best behavior. I didn't even mention that I was a pastor, too.

She made what I can only describe as chitchat about my cancer, while I swallowed off the nausea I could sense secreting in the back corners of my jaw. Compared with the Rituxan on my first night, my latest chemo-poison, methotrexate, felt downright merciful. At least it didn't stop me from fumbling my way through a conversation.

I knew it was time for the seminarian to take her leave when I saw her trying to glance at her watch without me noticing. I smiled and told her that not standing with my back to the clock on the hospital wall was one of the lessons I'd learned over the years. She responded with a confused smile and extended an invitation for the obligatory parting prayer, but first she asked me, "What stage is your cancer?"

When you have cancer, you learn how everyone wants to ask you about its stage. It's what movies, soap operas, and grapevine gossip have trained people to ask. I began explaining to her how traditional 1–5 staging was a poor measurement for my kind of cancer, but I could tell from her pained expression of empathy that I just sounded to her like I was in denial, that I was minimizing my malady.

"It's somewhere between stages 4 and 5," I gave up and told her.

Having given her the numbers, I suppose that's why she prayed the way she did.

Taking my hands in hers, which struck me as a presumptuous way to conclude a 240-second conversation, she closed her eyes and *smiled*, and after a pregnant pause, she prayed for me.

Thankfully, she spared me the Fatherwejust tripe I'd been expecting, and her prayer sounded surprisingly devoid of sentimentality, but dammit if her prayer wasn't all about me and *freaking eternal salvation* and me having the faith to trust myself to it.

It was only day three of my treatment. Eternity was the wrong number to throw at me.

My friend the poet-undertaker Thomas Lynch refers to eternity and our likelihood for it as the "Big One." In his book *The Undertaking: Life Studies from the Dismal Trade,* Tom writes:

> The Big One refers to the number of people out of every hundred born who will die. Over the long haul, The Big One hovers right around . . . well, dead nuts on one hundred percent.

> If this figure were on the [insurance] charts they'd call it death expectancy and no one would buy futures of any kind. But The Big One is a useful number and it has its lessons. Maybe it will make you want to figure out what to do with your life. Maybe it will make you hysterical with fear.

As a clergyman with a sizable chunk of my workaday year given over to beholding mysteries with a benediction and a fistful of dirt, I recognize the attention-getting power of a horizontal body. Indeed, I daresay, one horizontal body that's no longer moving is more compelling than two bodies that are moving horizontally together.

Like Tom, I know firsthand many times over that there's nothing quite like the presence of a dead guy to fix one's mind on figuring out lowest common denominators—namely, between you and the universe. Or God.

My trade as much as Tom's depends upon that number: the Big One. And for as long as I'd been a pastor, I'd operated on the assumption that the Big One—eternity, 100 percent death expectancy, 0 percent survival—is the only number that really matters in the grand scheme.

The Big One, I'd always thought, is the only number that matters for taking accounts, crediting real value, and putting life in its proper (read: spiritual) perspective.

But sitting there in the cancer ward, imbibing my cocktail of chemo-poison, I wasn't a pastor. Nor would I be for some time to come. I was a patient, and after one surprise surgery followed by a scary pant-pissing diagnosis, and facing a long chemo protocol that made me blanch and odds I'd rather not weigh, I became convinced that the Big One is not the only number that matters.

Not by a long shot.

In fact, as my first week of chemo progressed, numbers seemed to be the only thing I could wrap my head around. By day number 4 of something like 150 (*if* all goes well, said the doc) to come, I was feeling flatlined fatigued, tapped-out tired from my third twenty-four-hour drip of yet another "medicine" that ends with the unreassuring suffix -*toxin.*

Strapped to an IV pole, tethered by the port and tubes in my chest, and plugged into the wall, I felt like a plastic, beeping prisoner. And I've worked in a prison. I know of what I speak; prison is boring. The truth was, it had been only a couple of days, and I was already exhausted, a scorecard that made me swallow hard at the road ahead.

I was fed up with waiting to throw up. I was tired of waiting for when the meds would give me the runs, and I was tired of wondering whether I would be able to unplug all my equipment and make it to the toilet in time when they did. And I was seriously done with the way the brown-bagged potion on my IV pole made my piss the color of blood.

And burn at all my exit points.

Not to be too graphic.

My point is, I felt weary, and being wearied, I found that words were starting to prove elusive for me, making it easier for me to mark the time and transcribe the moments for my diary not in words but in numbers. Numbers like these:

- 43—the number of cancer-related television commercials I counted on day three during dinner

- 38—the number of those commercials that aired on CNN

- 24—the number of hours per day that *Crocodile Hunter* was on television

- 2006—the year *Crocodile Hunter*'s Steve Irwin died

- 7—the number of times the charge nurse bawled me out for refusing to wear the hospital-issue, rubberized, geriatric socks

- 3—the number of times the cancer-themed Joseph Gordon-Levitt/Seth Rogen bromance *50/50* aired during my first week of chemotherapy

- Too many to count—the number of tumors in my chest and abdomen regions, according to the CAT scan done on day two

- 5—the number of IV bags routed daily through the two tubes ported in my chest cavity

- 180—the number of seconds it took me to unplug all

those bags before I could begin to drag myself to the bathroom

- 13—the number of times I needed to get up to go to the bathroom every night

- 51—the number of minutes I spent crying, full-on tears, during lunch on day five while watching Charlie Rose interview a panel of New York oncologists

- 26—the number of minutes I made it into episode 1 of season 1 of *Breaking Bad* before realizing the premise hinged on a father and husband with terminal cancer, bawling like a strung-out meth-head, and turning it off

- 4—the number of times during our "walk" on day four that the soft-spoken licensed clinical social worker observed that I seemed "cynical"

- 3—the number of patients I could overhear weeping on my second night long past midnight

- 2—the number I overheard the next morning crying out in what sounded like agony while they threw up from their chemo

- 14—the number of times my doctor asked if I have diarrhea

- 8—the number of times I had had it

- 2—the number of times my mom surreptitiously washed my sharted-on shorts to spare me shame

- 23.6—the amount my white blood count dropped in my first few days of treatment

- 2—the number of panic attacks that awakened me in the middle of the night that week

- 19—the number of cans of Ensure, sent by the dietitian, that sat unopened in my room

- 75—the percentage of time I've not lived up to Ali's expectations

- 100—the percentage of time she's exceeded my own (OK, not really, but she's gotten pretty damn close)

- 52—the rough estimate of years, based on average life expectancy, I anticipated to have left with her

- 12—the age of my oldest son, the age I was when my parents split, an age I know can make a lifetime's difference

- 41—the percentage of my boys' lives I would miss while in treatment

- Forever—the amount of future time I assumed I had with them

- 35—the best-guess number of times that week I prayed a desperate, lame "Please, make it go away, God" prayer

- 0—the number of times God replied

With my brain cobwebbed on chemo and fitful sleep, I found it easier to mark the time in my journal with numbers. And sitting there in my bed, sifting through all those numbers and searching out lowest common denominators, I discovered that Tom's Big One wasn't the number that mattered most to me in the grand scheme.

Not anymore.

I didn't really give a damn about my 100 percent death expectancy anymore, because there were a few other numbers that had gripped my attention:

- 7—the median number of years for mantle cell lymphoma until a relapse occurs
- 44—the age my wife and I will be then
- 16—the age my youngest, Gabriel, will be when I cross that number
- 4—the number of years Ali and I will be just shy of our twenty-fifth anniversary
- 60—the decade to which my life expectancy is shortened if my MCL requires bone marrow transplants

Holding my hands, the chaplain-in-training said, "Amen," and opened her eyes. I'd never closed mine. She was still smiling.

I said, "Thank you for that."

But I was thinking, *I'd like to punch you in the teeth right now.*

Because I didn't care about eternity right then. I wasn't afraid to die. I didn't need a miracle or a cure, the latest elixir or a magic potion or the Jesus Prayer. I didn't need forever. I just wanted more time. That was all. Eternity was not a number I cared about, because I had numbers like seven and sixty that were now my Big Ones.

If there was one thing I had learned in this nearly monthlong nightmare, it's how quickly you can make peace with the likelihood you'll die far sooner than you expected, how quickly you can make peace with the fact that it's likely *this* that will kill you, how quickly you can make peace with it, *if* (a big effing if) you can just see your kids grow up, that's all.

You can make peace with the Big One, you tell yourself,

if you can just enjoy your spouse's company for another factor (or two) of seven.

Eternity felt like the wrong damn number to me because it's not so hard to make peace with death if you can just have a little bit more time.

So that's what I started to pray for that first week of treatment. More time.

Hopefully, it wasn't too much to ask for; after all, when you think about it, by returning to forgive the very people who did away with him, time—literally, all the time in the world—is the exact gift God gives us at Easter.

PASTORS MAKE BAD PATIENTS

Not only had I told them at Patient Registration that I was a Christian, I'd let slip to my first night-shift nurse that I was a pastor.

It had been a mistake, I decided almost instantly. If I were just another "Mister" instead of "Reverend," then I still would've been stuck there with a cancer as rare as a unicorn, but my week would've at least gone a bit better.

On day five, while I was sitting in my boxer-briefs, my gown twisted up around my waist, watching *19 Kids and Counting* and eating my Cinnamon Toast Crunch, a Filipino woman knocked on my door and then proceeded to wheel a large Zamboni-like machine into my hospital room.

"I'm here to take chest X-rays of you!" she said with more cheeriness than either the hour (7 a.m.) or the wing (oncology) required.

She did it all right there, pushing chairs and tables out of the way, positioning the machine directly in front of me, placing a block of wood behind my back for posture's sake, and a heavy flak jacket on my lap for safety.

Just before she started to snap pictures of my tumored chest, I said, "Hold on a minute. Is that machine going to give me . . . cancer?"

"No."

If you need empirical proof that the populace considers Christians to be uniformly unfunny, then a few days in the hospital should net all the data you need. That apparently goes doubly for leaders of the tribe.

In no time, I wished I'd snuck into the cancer ward seeking out chemo-poison the way Nicodemus sought out Jesus, by keeping my vocation—indeed, my faith—a secret. Because I didn't, every hospital employee seemed to assume that I was serious—deadly earnest—all the time. Nothing short of a knock-knock joke could break through the joyless, lugubrious stereotype they had for me and conveyed that in this instance (say, as I feign concern about cancer risks whilst receiving chemo on the oncology ward), I'm just screwing with you.

None of that time as a pastor among patients prepared me for how hard it was to be a pastor who was a patient. Five days into my first chemo bid, I discovered with the reliability of something like scientific law how pastors make bad patients.

It's at least as right as Murphy's law: pastors make bad patients.

As with many laws, the conditions that exemplify it are many, but chief among them is the widespread, apparently settled consensus that Christians in general and clergy in particular are about as funny as stage 4-to-5-ish cancer.

The gallows humor, sarcastic banter, and shit-happens philosophizing that would otherwise have made my days there more tolerable evaporated when everyone thought my M.O. as an R.E.V. is to be serious 100 percent of the time.

On my sixth night, after the woman from Dining Services had brought me my nineteenth unrequested can of chocolate-flavored Ensure, all of which remain unopened in my room, I told her, "Look, here, why don't you take this. There's actually a prohibition in Leviticus against mixing meatloaf with Ensure and fruit cocktail."

Blink. Blink.

(*Leaping to action*)

"Of course. I apologize, Father."

"Wait . . . what?!" I started to unwind my BS before deciding I'd end up making things worse.

Thus it had gone all that week.

"How are you feeling today?" asked the nurse one morning.

"Other than the rare, incurable cancer, I feel awesome today."

"Great!"

"On a scale of one to ten, ten being the max, what would you say your pain is this morning?"

(This just after the first night, when the chemo had given me convulsions that ripped open my stomach incision like it was a Hot Pocket.)

"Oh, I'm great. Definitely a zero this morning."

"That's fantastic!"

To spend a week there was not unlike having been raised by sarcastic wolves and suddenly being asked to pass for normal in civilization.

To the nurse drawing my blood one evening while I flipped channels on the TV: "Just how big would you say Nancy Grace's nostrils are? As big as racquetballs?"

Blink. Blink.

Straight face.

"Maybe five centimeters. Not nearly as big as a racquetball."

Life turns out not to be very much fun when everyone assumes you're no fun.

The verity of that maxim becomes exponentially clearer in the prison of the mind that insurance companies call hospitalization.

Before I received my last chemo infusion for that first cycle, the nurse prepped me with the caution that I should "refrain from both driving and sexual intercourse until the drugs have completely left your system."

Seriously.

Just like that, a fat one right over the plate.

"I guess that rules out having sex while I'm driving home then."

Blink. Blink.

Straight face.

"Yes. It does."

Not even a double take to see if I was being a wise ass.

"I guess I'll tell my wife she needs to make new plans," I mumbled to no reaction.

For me as a pastor, it was not easy being a patient if for no other reason than that everyone assumed I was more spiritual and less human than Jesus Christ himself.

My second night there, I asked my night-shift nurse for some concrete dos-and-don'ts advice about getting through my chemotherapy. She looked at me without pause and with something like a frown said, "Pray."

Not only was this not the sort of advice I wanted, the effect it had was to make me feel like my diagnosis was even more damned than I feared—as in, all someone in my shoes *can do* is pray.

And it was all because she knew—and she knew I knew she knew—that I'm a pastor. If I had been a short-order cook or an insurance adjuster or a thong model, she probably would've said, "Exercise thirty minutes a day," or, "Make sure you wash your vegetables." But instead, I got shit like "Pray." Which, on the face of it, was curious, since prayer was what everyone there assumed I was doing every waking moment anyway. One late afternoon, after all my visitors had left, I fell asleep reading in the armchair, and sure enough, the nurse tech who'd come to check my vitals immediately apologized for interrupting my prayer time.

"I wasn't praying; that's all right."

Blink. Blink.

And then she smiled—as if she didn't believe me, as if I'm such a model Christian I'm too humble even to admit to praying.

"No, seriously," I said. "I don't usually drool on myself when I'm praying. Well, actually, that's not true."

My bottom-line takeaway from my first week of treatment: It's hard to relate to people when they assume you're more perfectly human that they could ever hope for themselves, which, for a pastor, makes being a patient hard.

You hear about how doctors and nurses make bad patients, and I've always taken the reason to be procedural. Nurses know how the IV bags should be hung or the blood should be drawn. Doctors can read their lab results as well as their own doctor, and they know as well as them the alternative diagnoses and treatments available. Nurses and doctors make bad patients in the way my father-in-law makes a backseat driver or sports fans make obnoxious Monday-morning quarterbacks.

Their know-ledge and techniques of their trade make them bad patients. At least that's what I assumed. After a week as a patient, though, I wasn't so sure anymore. I wondered if instead doctors and nurses make bad patients because of exactly the same attribute they share with a pastor like me: memory.

As I said, I'd been a pastor for nearly fourteen years, and I'd spent a lot of time in hospitals. More specifically, I'd been a pastor at my most recent church for ten years, and in those ten years, I'd spent a lot of time in that very hospital.

For example, I could remember which babies were born in which rooms. I could recall what I half watched on the TV with which families as we waited for word in the ER or the OR. I could point down the hallways to the rooms for the suicides and the overdoses. And I could remember many of the folks with whom I had prayed who never made it home again, or did so only briefly as a sojourn on their way to a more eternal home.

After ten years, I could only recall a fraction of them. Still, the number was sufficiently high to make that place for me a haunted house, filled not with ghosts or specters but with emptiness. So many rooms and spaces there were just holes where people used to be.

Without exaggerating, I could close my eyes and turn right out of my room and turn right again out of my wing and right again to find the room where there was a mother I knew who lost both her legs to diabetes only a short while before she ultimately lost her life. And I couldn't tell you the exact room number, but I could take you to the place where, for weeks, a husband to his wife of more decades than I've lived read from the Psalms as she died of cancer.

I could drag my IV pole over to the ICU and show you the bed from which an every-Sunday worshipper (11:15 service, pulpit side, middle, third pew) never got up again. And from there, my slippered feet could take you to the PICU, where I spent the day with a couple nervously standing vigil by their boy's bedside. Their son, confirmed by me years ago, was only a few sizes and grades ahead of my eldest.

It was near that boy's room, on the fifth day of my chemo, where the licensed clinical social worker during our "walk" told me that I seemed "dark" to him. It was near there, where that boy nearly died, that I said in response to the social worker's observation, "No shit. Don't *you* work here?"

As a pastor, I turned out to be a bad patient because that place was for me what I'm sure it was for a lot of doctors and nurses, too: a tiled and antiseptic reminder, smelling vaguely of steamed vegetables and soiled linens, that life is so infuriatingly fragile.

Life is so fragile that, at times, the deepest faith in God can seem like insanity.

Doctors and nurses and pastors—we are all, as they say, in the "caring professions," which is just a jargoned euphemism to avoid admitting that death is a big part of what we do. Until I got cancer, I had been like a nurse who comes home wearing scrubs with someone else's bloodstains on them. It got close, but it still wasn't me or mine. But after ten years of being a pastor there—in *that* hospital—I was a patient there, and I found that I wasn't very good at the latter, entirely because of my experience with the former.

I couldn't look at my oncologist's data-driven poker face as he gazed at my most recent lab work without thinking of how I'd prayed with patients in half of the rooms on that same oncology unit, a memory that for whatever reason made me feel as if my odds run commensurate with those in the rooms I'd covered: fifty-fifty.

When I asked him why my swollen lymph nodes hadn't "totally disappeared," as he had promised they would by that point in my treatment, I didn't even really listen to the answer, because my mind drifted off, thinking of all those families I'd sat with as a pastor, listening as doctors promised a "full recovery" that never came—and in all likelihood never was going to come. We just didn't have ears to hear.

As a patient, I kept getting told that optimism and a positive frame of mind are constitutive of the healing process, but in more cases than I could remember, I knew, as a pastor, that seldom do either have anything to do with a cure.

God may be good and gracious, but you don't need to spend time as a pastor in a hospital to know that life is seldom fair or forgiving.

To patients.

And now I was one.

Now I was no different from anyone else, no different (and this was the real gist of it) from all those patients I'd visited as a pastor—many, if not most, of whom had since died.

It's amazing, counterintuitive even, how a daily proximity to death and all of its antecedents can actually give you a sense of invulnerability to it. If it's clichéd to say that the young think they're invincible, then it's doubly true for young pastors. I comfort and I counsel and I commit to the ground, dust to dust. In the midst of life, we're all ashes-in-waiting, I say. I witness to the resurrection, and I behold great mysteries, and I bury the dead until that day they put on imperishability.

I serve the suffering, but I do not suffer.

But now that I had cancer, I was like that guy in Mark's gospel story. I was the one with friends and loved ones willing to do anything, even cut a hole in the roof, if it would get Jesus to improve my prospects.

Now I was the diseased one on the mat.

And to be as honest as I've ever been about anything: I hated the view.

It's funny—when you're a pastor, you think about scripture passages like the one where Jesus asks the begrudgers, "Which is easier to say? Your sins are forgiven or get up, take your mat, and walk?" and you imagine that it's a loaded question.

Clearly, we're meant to see that forgiveness is the harder miracle to broker. Healers were a dime a dozen throughout the 'burbs and backwoods of first-century Israel. There was nothing special about healings in Jesus' day, so there is nothing unique about Jesus who performs them. Many healed, but only Jesus offers forgiveness.

And therein lies the predictable preacher's lesson for the day: more precious than any doctor's "all clear" should be the assurance from our loved ones, from enemies or exes past, or from God in the person of our priest that things, relationally speaking, are all clear—that our sins are forgiven, wrongs blotted out, and resentments set aside.

Once I became a cancer patient, however, I began to wonder if my preacher's reading of such stories wasn't too cute by half. Now that I was a patient, with a rare cancer whose odds of survival made me look not much luckier than the poor bastard on the mat, it no longer struck me as a loaded question. Not at all.

Sure, in the seven days I lay there in the cancer ward, feeling nauseated and depressed and hurting, I gave plenty of thought to the relationships I'd let fray and the wounds I'd let fester for what, in hindsight, seemed no good reasons at all.

Sure, forgiveness was important, and, yes, I believed Jesus offers it.

But you know what Jason the Patient on the mat discovered that Pastor Jason, standing in the pulpit, had not? Healing's important, too—damn important. And, whether this thought is heresy or not, healing is no less a miracle than forgiveness.

"Which is easier to say? Your sins are forgiven or get up, take your mat, and walk?"

What I hadn't realized before as a pastor is this: Jesus' words are not a loaded question. It turns out that both are hard to say and harder still to pull off, and neither is possible apart from the grace of God in Christ.

Grace, as every pastor knows, is by definition undeserved and, thus, unpredictable. And knowing that, as a pastor, made me a piss-poor patient.

CANCER HAS ITS USES; FAITH NOT SO MUCH

In spite of everything, I felt determined that cancer would not be all weeping and gnashing of IV ports. Even if no one thought I was funny, I'd keep on trying to milk cancer for all of its potential.

My last night in the cancer ward, Ali, having visited me for much of the evening, got up to go home and put our boys to bed. Smiling tenderly, she leaned over my hospital bed to kiss me good-bye. She put her hand on my cheek, gentle and soft, and I put mine on her waist. Her hand remained there on my cheek, as true and chaste as a Jane Austen heroine. Meanwhile, mine—left and right—wandered gently upward, just enough to cop a feel of her . . . ahem.

"How many times in twenty years have I told you not to do that?!" she chastised me.

Me, adopting a confused look, as if I were trying to do the sum of all those times previous in my head: "But honey . . . I have cancer."

It almost worked.

The morning of my discharge, my first round of treatment behind me, I learned they were going to release me with a prescription for a medication for vaginal yeast infections and herpes. Cancer may have riddled my body with tumors too many to count, gotten me to pray desperate prayers for more time, and exposed me as a terrible, odds-weighing patient, but it also handed me humor gold like herpes and vagina pills.

I had my parting shot to Joyce, my favorite nurse: "Herpes?! Herpes!? No wonder I was sleeping so fitfully! What were you ladies doing with me while I was unconscious?!"

Joyce blushed. She shook her head at me and then cackled despite herself when I mock-accused her.

Cancer, I smiled to myself, *has its uses.*

People think faith is like that. Useful. Especially when the poop hits the biopsy. It all goes back to Freud, who famously said that religion is "born from man's need to make his helplessness tolerable." Even unbelievers assume that faith is useful for calming your nerves, helping you to cope with the fears and anxieties that come when the

CT scan shows objectively that the Grim Reaper is taking a long, hard gander at you.

Just the day before, my licensed clinical social worker at the hospital, having told me how enamored he was with Eastern traditions, had presented "Buddhist meditation techniques" to me as a potentially positive "healing tool."

Tools, we all know, are designed to be nothing if not useful.

From the hundreds of cards and e-mails and prayers I received during my week of treatment, I noticed just how many people presumed that faith, too, is useful for pondering the big, cosmic questions that accompany terminal diagnoses. Faith is useful, so the canard goes in many a sympathy card, for justifying the goodness and reliability of God's ways when the world appears otherwise ambivalent. Faith is useful, the sleeves-rolled-up advice to me went, for finding God's benevolence amidst the malevolence wracking your life.

Faith, in other words, is useful not just for alleviating anxiety; it's also useful for supplying answers to mysteries too dark to leave without rebuttal. Maybe that's the way faith works for some people. In fact, I'm absolutely certain that's how faith works for many people.

But not me.

For me, faith isn't like that.

Faith doesn't provide a shot of optimism or a push of positive thinking, for faith in the cross and resurrection isn't optimism; it's against-all-odds, in-the-face-of-all-just-merit hope. Faith isn't like all the steroid chasers to my chemo-poisons, convincing me I can lick cancer because I've the Big Guy in my corner for the bout of my life. Cancer may have its practical benefits, but I'm not so sure faith does—at least, not in the way we typically imagine benefits.

Contrary to what most people assumed, my faith did not at all comfort me in the days of my first chemo cycle. It didn't help me sleep easier at night, and it sure as hell did not silence the abacus in the back of my brain always doing the odds before me. Nor did my faith provide any easy answers or assurances. Freud was wrong. My faith, I discovered, was not any kind of coping mechanism.

When you have stage-serious cancer, you realize how everyone assumes a rare, aggressive cancer diagnosis will beget the "Why me, God?" question à la the Book of Job, which in a few short weeks I had decided is a thoroughly dissatisfying story because Job never encounters anyone who's hurting as much as he is.

Surprisingly, cancer doesn't lead you to ask Job's question any more than faith arms you with his answers. What cancer does is thrust you into a community of people you didn't know existed—people who are hurting every bit as much, if not more than, you.

For example, there was a girl on my oncology ward. She was twenty-three and the mother of a two-week-old. She learned she had cancer—had it bad—during her delivery. I listened to her cry every night when they came to bring me my night meds.

The nurse I spoke to at my oncologist's office, just before I started chemo, said I was one of thirty people she was scheduled to see that day alone. People of all shapes and sizes and situations. And ages.

Cancer doesn't make you wonder, "Why me, God?" Only a dick would get caught up with that kind of question. No, cancer throws in you the scrum and makes you ask, "Why them, God?"

Why *us*, God? Why this world? Which is the only possible world if the world, as my faith teaches me, is indeed the perfect expression of God's infinite goodness. Why this world where a lion fulfilling its lion-ness leads to the lamb being slaughtered and where a few efficient tumorous cells fulfilling their design lead to cancer?

That was my problem with the book of Job, the Old Testament folktale in which God devastates Job with the loss of his family and home and afflicts him with painful illness in order to determine whether Job loves God for God's own sake or because God had blessed Job with such an abundant life. As a preacher, I've never cared for the book of Job. The morality play nature of it makes God seem like an arbitrary prick, and when God does finally show and speak to Job from the whirlwind, God can't bother to answer any of Job's pained, plaintive questions. With cancer, I discovered I disliked the book of Job for different reasons. For one, Job's cast of characters is too small; the point of view is too limited. Job never so much as goes to the doctor's office. Job never encounters anyone who is suffering as much as he is.

Cancer doesn't lead you to ask, "Why me, God?" Cancer leads you to wonder why God, whom we call Light, can't seem to enter or act in our world without casting shadows.

Faith wasn't comforting or practical for me. For me, faith was more like that story where Jesus needs a do-over before healing a blind man. After Jesus' initial try, the man says, "I see people . . . but they look like trees walking." Faith was like that for me as I underwent chemo; faith was to have been touched by Christ only to have the world appear more bewildering than when I was blind. Like that story, faith got me wondering why God doesn't seem to have gotten everything right in the first go-round.

Faith amidst my suffering instead put me in mind of others' suffering, reminding me that Christ's suffering wasn't isolated or even unique. Rather, somehow summarized in Christ's suffering and encompassed by it was the suffering of all those others who were crucified on the same day as he was. Faith was not useful, not in the sense my licensed clinical social worker encouraged.

Cross-shaped faith doesn't cultivate a positive, productive attitude. It produces hatred, perfect hatred, toward the meaningless of all suffering, the absolute needlessness of sin, and the sheer unnatural emptiness of death, which the first Christian proclamation outs as our "last enemy."

So while cancer proved useful in giving me dozens of jokes about my vagina, faith didn't work for me in a similarly productive fashion.

What faith gave me is more like what my teacher David Bentley Hart calls a *posture*, knowing that, in the suffering, dying faces I saw in the oncologist's office and there on the cancer ward, I did not see the face of God.

Instead I saw God's enemy, Death, against which the cross and empty tomb enlist my meager help. That's not exactly "useful." But as we say in the church, it is the gospel.

The night after my surgery, while we waited for a word for the type of cancer in my body, I wrote this question and answer on my blog as a part of an online catechism I'd been writing:

Question 13: How should we speak of God?

With deep humility, realizing that even our best speech is

nonsense when applied to God and, as sinners, we're prone to project our feelings and wills upon God.

We should speak of God always realizing our best words fit God like a baby's clothes fit on a grown-up. Our language for God is approximate without being at all adequate. For this reason, the best way to speak of God is to begin by saying what God is not (an approach called the *via negativa*):

> God is not hate, for example.
>
> God is not a man with a beard.
>
> Or, God is not cancer.

When we arrive at a negative statement which we know is false (e.g., "God is not Love"), then we know we've hit upon something true.

CHAPTER 4.

SIDE EFFECTS

In the days after I finished my first A cycle, as my blood counts and immune system fell exponentially each day in response to the chemo, I consulted my image in the bathroom mirror and imagined what I would find there once my hair fell out. I'd usually pray before I opened my eyes to the mirror.

Would I look like Captain Jean-Luc Picard/Professor Francis Xavier? I wondered. Or, with my earring and damsel-distressing muscles, maybe I'd be able to go trick-or-treating as Mr. Clean. *Once I'm bald and my beard is gone, what are the chances,* I mused hopefully, *I'll get mistaken for Billy Corgan, the front man for the Smashing Pumpkins?* Whenever I posited the possibilities that alopecia might bring, my son Gabriel, ever helpful, would shake his head and tell me I would probably look like a villain—Lex Luthor, he supposed.

My hair fell out in chunks nearly as fast as the previous few weeks had felt.

After it did, I joked to my boys that I looked like Mr. Bigglesworth, the cryogenically hairless cat from *Austin Powers.* They laughed only a little. I could tell from the concerned way they kept looking at me that I didn't look like The Rock or The Transporter. I just looked like I had cancer.

My oncologist had prepared me for the chemo's side effects. Returning home from the cancer ward, I anticipated the diarrhea and nausea brought on by the toxins, the constipation caused by the antinausea drugs, and the hunger provoked by the steroids. I expected my hair to fall out as my healthy cells died right along with my cancerous cells. I knew my risk of infection climbed as my white blood cells cratered, and I'd been told my thinning red blood cells would leave me dizzy and short of breath.

The one side effect no one warned me about was what people would say to me when they found out I had cancer. With cancer, I caused side effects in others in a way that reminded me of one late morning when I was lifeguarding at my neighborhood pool as a teenager. Like the time I accidentally saw my Italian great-grandma, who possessed a steelworker's mustache, naked, the moment is seared into my memory. At a quarter to some hour, (hard-bodied) teenage me blew my whistle long and low to clear the pool for break. Climbing down off my stand, I noticed a girl, maybe ten years old, bouncing and splashing around in the middle of the pool, evidently without any urgency or intention of exiting.

A relatively new Christian, I decided to be patient and kind, as I'd read Saint Paul suggest in my NIV Study Bible, but after fetching the kit from the pump house and testing the pH level of the water, I noticed that the little girl was still bouncing around the pool nowhere near a ladder or the steps.

I marched the circumference of the deck to the point

nearest her and then slowly, with no little drama, placed two exasperated hands on the waistband of my red lifeguard suit.

"Hey, you, little girl. I'm talkin' to you," I said with clipped Travis Bickle affect. "I said *clear the pool.* It's break time."

"I know," she responded as though the fact that she knew was the most obvious thing in the world.

"You know, huh? Well then," I said, exasperated, "*why* are you still in the pool? What are you, blind or something?"

"Yes," she said simply. "I *am* blind."

I'm a big believer in odds, and the odds of this happening to me just didn't seem possible.

"What?" I said.

"I am blind," she said again without contempt.

Ugh. Gut punch.

I could feel the red rapidly spreading across my face and through my eyes.

Her lack of malice made me feel all the more awful, so much so I said nothing.

Just to populate the scene for you: Sitting within earshot of this exchange were five moms from church, tanning themselves in too-tiny two-pieces, their Liz Claiborne sunglasses now perched on top of their foreheads so they could stare at me and, I assumed in a second, report back to the congregation. Meanwhile, no more than twelve inches behind me, six of my closest friends sat around an umbrellaed picnic table. One of those six I hoped soon to make my girlfriend, a wager I now assumed was about as likely as, well, asking a random girl if she was blind and hitting on "yes" in reply.

Eventually, in a tone of voice shamed low, I guided

her to the ladder, where she said, "Thank you," and I did not—I should confess—say, "I'm sorry." It was an eternity that lasted not much more than a few minutes. Still, it was one of those awkward-in-the-bowels, nothing-can-ever-undo-it moments when everyone within earshot wishes they could hide or die or flux-capacitor it back an hour.

Now—

Picture *me* as that blind girl, and you have some idea of what it was like when people found out that I had cancer.

WHAT PEOPLE SAY WHEN YOU HAVE CANCER

As a result of my chemo, I became neutropenic; that is, my white blood cells zeroed out, leaving me with no immune system to fight off even the most everyday of infections. So while I remained fairly sequestered inside my home, I still suffered plenty of those uncomfortable, you-really-stepped-in-it moments.

The awkward, cringe-inducing moments usually began thusly:

"How are you?"

"Uh . . . OK . . . fine. I'm fine."

"Really? You look . . . thinner? Have you lost weight?"

"Um . . . yeah . . . maybe a bit. Well, . . . the thing is, . . . I have cancer."

The pregnant pause that followed as reliably as the earth revolves around the sun usually gave birth to one or more clichés lying dormant at the mind's ready:

"You're young and healthy. You'll beat it," many assured me. Whether they were attempting to convince me or themselves varied by the person.

"Healthy except for the tumors squatting all over my body," I always replied, sometimes silently.

Some responded to the pregnant pause by delivering

up, either as an article of faith or something gleaned from first- or second- or usually third-hand experience, "Well, I believe in the power of prayer."

Many tried to turn the foreboding cloud of cancer inside out by pointing vaguely to the silver lining of "advances in medicine and science."

Some intended either the former (faith) or the latter (science) when they promised me in palliative tones that "miracles *do* happen," as though the prognosis I preferred to hear was how my full recovery was about as likely as feeding an entire hospital with just six pieces of Wonder bread and two fillets of poorly breaded tilapia.

I could tell from their faces and from what they tossed back at me: Being hit unawares with the C-word is like learning you've just been making sarcastic blindness cracks at a little blind girl. Nearly everyone stammered and then moved to tell me which Dr. Oz–endorsed books I should read or which cancer-fighting foods I should purchase at Whole Foods for five thousand dollars per pound.

Those less burdened by propriety or self-consciousness immediately asked how often I was throwing up or, I kid you not, "getting it up." Still others suggested cancer-themed movies I should watch, like Michael Keaton's forgotten film *My Life* or Bette Midler's wish-we-could-forget-it *Beaches*.

No one told me about the side effects cancer patients cause.

I held onto my beard and eyebrows a little longer than my hair, but as soon as they fell out, too, the C-word became harder to avoid. A week after I'd finished my first A cycle, I sat in the sun in my front yard, reading. I noticed the little black hairs from my chin on the page of my book just as door-to-door salesmen from Capitol Meats pulled into my driveway.

Upon hearing I had cancer (yes, I was playing the cancer card to avoid buying a gross of ground beef), one said, "Damn, man . . . that [effing] sucks." And then he added, "You should watch that movie. . . . What's it called? . . . ," and then he started to snap his fingers to jog his memory. "*Ordinary People*. Yeah, that's a damn good movie."

"It is a good one," I said. "But I'm pretty sure it's not a cancer movie."

"Nah, man," the meat man maintained. "Dude definitely dies of cancer in it."

Not every conversation went down like the blind girl in the pool, but once I'd blindsided people with the C-word and they'd recovered enough to respond with the typical clichés, recommendations, or curiosities, they then would usually ask me the same question:

"What kind of cancer?"

And once I told them, "Lymphoma. Mantle cell lymphoma," unless I was speaking to a doctor or a nurse, that marked the end of their oncological knowledge, so inevitably they would steer the conversation to the biographical.

"My mother / father / aunt / uncle / coworker / neighbor / cousin had lymphoma," they'd say, as though we were discussing fellow frat brothers from faraway chapters.

"Really?" I'd feign interest. "How did — do with their treatment?"

"Oh . . . um . . . he/she did . . . ," and then nine out of ten times, their voice would trail off in such a way that I was led to only one conclusion.

That's just freaking awesome.

The Friday before my surgery, the Friday after the night I'd learned cancer was the most likely culprit behind my troubles, my mom and I sat at the Y watching my boys at swim practice. My mom broke our own kind of pregnant pause: "You know . . . my uncle [as in my grandma's flesh-and-blood brother] had lymphoma, too."

"What? Really?" I said. "I didn't know that; I guess I should have checked the cancer box under 'Family History,' along with heart disease and mental illness."

"What happened to him?" I asked after she didn't laugh.

"Oh," she said, brainstorming how to change the subject. "Um . . . uh . . . er . . . yeah, he died."

"Great, just great," I said.

She went on: "But he lived a long time—at least until his midforties."

Midforties?! Midforties!? Geez, Mom, that's some cold shit.

When I spoke to the suit in the United Methodist Pension Office about my application for medical disability, he told me in a way that defied his bean-counting countenance, "I'm sorry to hear about your . . . uh . . . situation. I had a college roommate who died of lymphoma."

"I'm very sorry to hear that," I said, suddenly wondering who was supposed to be comforting whom.

"Yeah, he was such a great guy." And just then I thought our connection had gone, before I realized he was sniffling into the phone. Then he started weeping.

Likewise did it go with the insurance rep who called to audit my care plan. My lymphoma, though a rarer breed, apparently put her mind to her own mother's losing bid against blood cancer.

Not only did the C-word provoke people into

unwittingly portending my death, it was also—*I was also*—a grim reminder of painful mournings of their own.

In other words, now that I had cancer, I ripped the scabs off of people's wounds.

One side effect of cancer was the side effects I had on others.

For those without family or friends felled by blood cancer, a surprising number of people, upon hearing my news, turned for reference to America's family of choice, i.e., celebrities.

"Oh, did you know Jackie Onassis died of lymphoma?" the kid at the Safeway checkout told me a few days after I completed my first A cycle.

Really? Before, I was worried, but now that I know Jackie O died of it, I think, "What's the big deal?" I thought to myself before stretching a fake smile across my face and nodding solemnly. *I mean, thank God I have blood cancer and not some peasant disease like COPD*, I kept thinking to myself as I punched my debit number into the screen.

I now knew that Charles Lindbergh, Gene Autry, and Joey Ramone of the Ramones all died of the very affliction that was now doing its damnedest to kill me.

There's something about the word *cancer* that throws a wrench into most people's mental gears.

When I told that same Capitol Meats salesman that I was no longer working, that I was going on disability (because, yes, I was playing the cancer card to get rid of him and his sales pitch), he immediately responded by telling me, "Yeah, one of my cousins on my mama's side is retarded. He's real sweet, though. You can hardly tell he's retarded."

I just nodded along and smiled, which probably only confirmed for him that I, too, was disabled as his sweet cousin—which, fortunately, in his mind probably disqualified me from making such a hefty purchase of boneless steaks and pork chops.

————————

Some people see *cancer* as a two-syllable body bag, one that was already zipped up to around my chest port. To their minds, it gave off an air of the inexorable that permitted them to confess secrets they'd never reveal otherwise.

In those first weeks of cancer, (sometimes long-lost) acquaintances would message me the stuff normally reserved for eulogies:

- "You were my first crush."
- "I never told you what your friendship meant to me."
- "I thought you were a real dick in high school, but I'm sending you positive energy now."
- "I thought you were the worst preacher I'd ever heard for about five years, but now I think you're awesome."

One person, upon hearing the news via the social-media grapevine, sent me a copy of the poem "Do Not Stand by My Grave and Weep," verses that I not only loathe but have only ever heard intoned—against my better judgment—at *funerals.*

Of all the various and sundry responses the news of my stage-serious cancer elicited, by far the most common responses were these:

- "Fight it."
- "It's time to do battle."

- "Kick cancer's ass."

From their shoes, I think they were exactly the right things to say. It sure as hell beat telling me that Bob Ross died of lymphoma (too). After all, "Kick cancer's ass" wasn't burdened with any pray-it-away piety or false promises, and it put the onus on me while positioning the speaker as being behind me, in my corner, rooting for me in the fight of/for my life.

Yeah, kick cancer's ass, I sometimes nodded my head in response.

But here was the real difficulty: The *it* in "Fight it, Jason" was Jason. The *it* was me—indelibly me. The cancerous cells were mine, only doing something differently (and far more efficiently) than my healthy ones. The chromosomes inverting themselves way down deep in my marrow, which is what gives me *mantle cell* lymphoma—those were *my* chromosomes. They were as much me as my eyes or my fingerprints or the corner of my lips that produces my smile.

The tumors riddling my insides—they were attached to my spleen and my stomach and my lungs and God knows what else, and it was my lymphatic system that so conveniently delivered those tumorous cells to the rest of my body and possibly my brain (one of the unique perks of mantle cell).

What I only realized now that I had cancer was that the problem with "Fight it" was that cancer isn't an alien, external opponent to be defeated. The masses were in me—a part of me even. "It" was also very much me. Which means, of course, that the only way to kick cancer's ass was to kick my own.

DOING CANCER IN THE PASSIVE VOICE

Normally at that time of year, Lent, I would be giving up meat or booze or Facebook, but that Lent, though I had not chosen it, I was doing something even more Christ-like, in a way. I was forsaking myself. Don't applaud me. It was out of necessity, not any piety. It's just the way chemo works. The only way to kill the cancer in me was to let the doctors get as damn close as they could to killing me. Like somewhere in between "Why, O why, have you forsaken me, O God?" and "Then he breathed his last."

I was learning quickly how there's an inherent passivity to cancer, no matter how proactive and intentional I might've wanted to be against it. For much of the year to follow, I was literally a prisoner of my body. On a cellular level, my body echoed Saint Paul: "For I do not do the good I want to do, but the evil I do not want to do—this I keep on doing." My body was exhibit B for Alfred Lord Tennyson's contention that the biological we so often gush over as beautiful is actually "red in tooth and claw."

This is why those with cancer so desperately need others—especially doctors and nurses—because no sane person, no matter how sick or scared, would ever willingly do to him- or herself what treatment requires. The regimen of chemo-poison is as harrowing as it is painful.

I still appreciate the sentiment behind "Kick cancer's ass," but I've learned that the language of fighting doesn't really work for cancer. It's too active; in fact, I don't believe the active voice really works at all for cancer.

I don't believe the active voice works for cancer for the

same reasons I don't believe the active voice doesn't work for God.

I remember one preaching class when I was in seminary. A belligerently confident, hyper-evangelical classmate preached his sample sermon before the class, and it was frenetic. He clearly thought he was the superior preacher to all of us, and admittedly, his delivery was effective. However, our professor looked restless and irritated through the entirety of the twenty minutes. Once the student finished, the professor breathed out his exasperation and asked, "Do you realize not one of your sentences had God as its subject?"

Contrary to all the Strunk and White rules, when it comes to our speech about God, specifically about ourselves *in relation to* God, the passive voice is most often the best, for it alone conveys the necessity of our trust and dependence upon God, who is necessarily the subject of the sentences we call our lives. The active voice makes it sounds like we actually have our shit together and just need God to show up sometimes. But the passive voice confesses, "You can do, God, what we cannot." The passive admits more clearly that when it comes to things that matter, like sin and marriage and parenthood and friendship and truth telling and compassion and cancer, most often my enemy is myself. The passive voice better points out that in much of life, but particularly with cancer, the path forward looks not like active ass-kicking at all but instead something in between resignation and resistance, because that's the space where God goes.

The word the Gospels use to describe such passivity is *possession*. There's a story in Mark's Gospel about a Gerasene man possessed by a demon. Having been ostracized by his community, he was pushed out to the margins of society, left to wander among the graveyard tombs, dragging behind him the bits of broken chains with which his neighbors had once tried to bind him. The possessed man bows before Jesus and addresses him, despite his affliction, as "Son of the Most High God." Jesus heals him and casts his tormentors into a herd of pigs.

Enlightened, credentialed preachers like me never take a story like that one straight up. Almost blushing from the pulpit, we instead bend over backward, doing exegetical gymnastics, to qualify what we take to be a supernatural story with primitive assumptions behind it. *We all know in this day and age that illnesses aren't caused by demons* is our implicit starting point. Except, being stage-serious sick with cancer feels exactly like possession, like having a malevolent intruder within you, pushing you to the margins of the life you knew, powerless to exorcise and unbind yourself.

All of which is to say, as much as I would've liked to "fight it" or "kick cancer's ass," my only real hope was that God would be in me, too, setting things right, just as scripture promises God was in Christ, reconciling all things to himself.

Rather than active-voice, ass-kicking determination, cancer brings you to the same conclusion as Jürgen Moltmann, surveying the cross: only the crucified God, who has shared your fear, suffering, and humiliation and made your pain his own, can help.

PRAY WHEN YOU'RE HEALTHY

My particular chemo, R-HyperCVAD, was a cocktail of poisons with Dr. Moreau names like cyclophosphamide, vincristine, doxorubicin, dexamethasone, methotrexate, cytarabine, and rituximab. You know they're bad when the handouts tell you to double flush after going to the bathroom, for fear that your dog might drink the water and die.

My chemo would be given to me for a week at a time in eight alternating cycles every twenty-one days. Those days would get longer, the doctor warned, if my body's recovery got slower.

Developed at the MD Anderson Cancer Center for "use in treatment of serious and aggressive forms of hematological malignancy . . . and reserved for young, fit patients because of its intensity," my chemo protocol, in just a few short weeks, recast my self-image from Clint Eastwood to Rick Moranis. Everyone had the cliché backward: cancer kicked my ass. And it did so quickly.

Along the course of ministry, you overhear tidbits of wisdom that, like stones against the wind and the sea, with the passage of time acquire the sheen of something like the absolute. The Truth. One such folk koan came to me by way of Fred Holly some fourteen years earlier. Fred was an elderly parishioner at the tiny New Jersey church where I served as a part-time pastor. It was the sort of church where the term *elderly parishioner* was redundant.

A curmudgeonly sort, Fred let it be known often that he only attended worship out of the habit enforced by his wife; never mind that the late Mrs. Holly had left the earth around the same time Fred's beloved Tricky Dick had left the White House. Since then, Fred had been unfailing in complaining about his Sunday obligation. And he was vocal in his assessment that my "only attribute worth a damn [was] my sexy dame of a wife."

In the first spring of my ministry, I visited Fred in the intensive-care unit of a Bucks County hospital. The day before, he'd had a bypass done on more of a heart than

I thought he possessed. His hair was mussed and greasy. His eyes looked small and round—mole-like. His gown hung down off his beefy shoulders like a cotton evening dress. When I walked in, he was sitting up in bed, a large teddy bear in his lap. Whenever he breathed or coughed, he clutched the teddy bear against the incision that ran from his groin to his collar. And every time he'd grimace, red-faced and veined, the agony in his expression was in inverse proportion to the blank, serene visage of the bear.

After one painful coughing fit that ended with a long, thunderous yawp of a fart (which seemed to amuse him), Fred wiped the sweat from his forehead and said, "Jesus, goddamn, Rev, I'll tell you what: Get all your prayin' in when you're healthy. It's just too damn hard to pray when you're busted up and sick."

And right then and there, it struck me as true and sound in the way of other sayings like "Never eat yellow snow" or "Don't play leapfrog with a unicorn" or "Sharing your medical info is always more embarrassing when it's shared with a moderately attractive nurse-practitioner of your approximate age."

His statement had the ring of a proverb, even though I've not heard it elsewhere and had not returned to it since. Not until cancer started kicking my ass. Conventional wisdom and all, you might just as easily expect it to be the opposite, but Fred was right: Praying is hard when you're busted up and sick.

During my first A Cycle of chemo-poison, after one of my several "walks" with the earnest licensed clinical social worker, my slippered feet found their way to the hospital chapel. Having listened to the LCSW spout new-agey and not-a-little-patronizing ideas about mindfulness and Zen meditation, contrarian-me determined to do some old-school, Holy Roman, hegemonic praying.

I knew the hospital had a chapel, because I'd seen it on the constant, twenty-four-hour live camera stream on the hospital's uppermost television channel, just after the porny Latin soap opera station. It was like the National Zoo's panda cam without the pandas; every time I flipped past it to get to Wolf Blitzer or *19 Kids and Counting*, the chapel was always empty.

So I wasn't surprised when I opened the chapel door, dragged my IV pole in behind me, and found the little sanctuary empty. Like such spaces in airports and colleges and funeral homes everywhere, the chapel was so enthusiastically ecumenical as to be bland. It felt more like a little nook at a Courtyard Marriott. Nonetheless, I sat down in the front row, my chemo my only companion, and attempted to pray in the manner of the saints and martyrs before me.

Later that evening, when the young Muslim woman from Food Services brought me my chicken soup and Ensure, her eyes brightened, and smiling, she said, "I saw you on the TV! In the chapel! A patient down the hall turned the channel when I picked up his lunch tray earlier today."

"You saw me?"

She nodded and smiled and added, "Poor thing, you must be exhausted."

I must've looked confused.

"The Muslim way is better," she explained. "It's harder to fall asleep when you're on your knees."

The little fact of stage-serious cancer notwithstanding—and I realize this is a bit like Larry Flynt confessing he's just not that into women—the Xrated truth of the matter is that I've never been very good at prayer.

In the same way that for a time in college I could participate in a conversation in French class about the meaninglessness of existence, *le jazz*, or American imperialism, I know *how* to pray. But prayer has never been anything like my first language.

Being a duly ordained Reverend (as in "one to be revered"), I can pray. I can *do* it in a performative, professional manner, but in the same way I can summon something resembling etiquette for a formal dinner, even this is not my natural or most comfortable posture. Honestly, even with the little self-awareness I possess, I know that I'm vain enough, despite being introverted, to lap up the approval and adoration of an audience; consequently, I've always maintained a healthy skepticism regarding public prayer, both my own and others'.

But the bottom line is, healthy or very much not healthy, I'm a piss-poor pray-er. I get restless. I get bored, and bored, I get distracted. If only God had an e-mail address or a Twitter account or had a regular coffee shop hangout, because closed eyes and bowed head seldom works for me. "Quiet time" sounds to me exactly like it sounds to my nine-year-old: punishment—or at least something to be endured.

Even worse than the boredom that makes you feel incompetent at prayer is the sudden rushing awareness of how superficial is most of your prayer. That leaves you feeling inauthentic—incomplete as a human being.

And then there are those days—more frequent than most pastors will admit—when you're convinced that you're mistaken about God, about Christ, about everything else in the creed. Cancer coaxes such questions at a stronger clip. On those days, prayer especially can feel like 100-proof superstition, making you feel the fool.

Given my own dissatisfying experience with prayer, when I found myself sick and/or dying and people told me they were praying for me (which everyone did, and I'm grateful), I felt guilty—guilty that my cancer had laid this extra burden upon them that would only lead to them feeling restless or bored or distracted or superstitious and, thus, foolish.

My track record with and previous affections for prayer in no way canceled out the verities I heard in that Bucks County ICU. What was hard and unnatural for me before was damn near impossible after cancer staged a hostile takeover of my body, my blood, and my family's life.

I walked away from more than a few prayers in my first weeks with cancer, because Fred was dead-on.

For my second CT scan, which was done my first week of chemo to see if I had any tumors in my upper body like the ones latched onto me all over my lower body (I did), I tried to pray the Lord's Prayer as I grimaced against my stomach incision, raised my arms over my head, and lay still as the camera spun around my chest.

I couldn't remember all the words.

Temptation.

Trespass.

Daily bread and deliverance.

As the giant camera spun around me, I kept getting the phrasing in the wrong order. I've led the Lord's Prayer at least a thousand times on Sundays alone, but without the backing chorus of a congregation behind me, my rhythm was off. I tried many times after then to recite it, mostly in the gray hours when the night sweats or the urgent need to piss out the poisons left me wide awake. I always screwed it up. Likewise Psalm 23, another prayer that in my former life I knew by heart.

Speaking of the psalms, now that I had cancer and couldn't pray worth a damn, I became amazed that King David, what with his turbulent TMZ life and all, was able to compose as many prayers as he did. David may be the exception that proves Fred's rule.

Before my first CT scan, done at my GI doctor's orders, I didn't pray at all; I hadn't thought there was a need to pray. I didn't think there was anything, save a gallstone or two, wrong with me, certainly not the C-word.

I prayed *during* that first CT scan, however. The radiology tech had given me an injection of contrast, which as a side effect would give me a warm, wet sensation all over my body, none of which—*and this is key*—he told me beforehand. So lying there, unsuspecting under a sheet, my pants pulled down around my ankles, an awareness suddenly and mercilessly washed over me: "Oh. My. God. I just crapped my pants."

In the same way there are (supposedly) no atheists in foxholes, this realization immediately gave way to supplication: "Please, God, let it not be bad. Please, God, let me get out of here without too many people noticing, especially not the cute receptionist at the front desk."

It was some kind of prayer, to be sure.

Later that night, when the GI doctor called me and asked, "Are you sitting down?" I was too scared to pray.

Jesus, facing death in the garden in John's Gospel, prays for pages upon pages upon pages. I suppose that's the difference between being God incarnate and just being carnate.

Studying the Hebrew Bible in college and seminary, I learned the "proper" form of prayer, beginning with a broad address to God, some name that hits at the highlights of God's résumé, and then moving on to praise God for God's gracious acts in salvation history, and then—and only then—beseeching God to do likewise for you today.

It's a lesson I've reinforced with confirmation classes, organizing prayers like study notes, with the acronym P-T-A: Praise, Thank, and only then Ask.

Such niceties are just that: nice. But they're all but impossible when you feel yourself salivating fear in the corners of your jaw or when you're just bone-marrow tired. Fred Holly was right. A major side effect of my sickness, I found, was my inability to pray. And what made the praying hard wasn't so much that God was absent; it was that the pain and the fear and the fatigue seemed more present to me than God.

Most of my post-diagnosis prayers more closely resembled my adolescent, pre-Christian prayers:

- Please let me get an A on this quiz.
- Please may the Reds beat the A's in the World Series.
- Please makes these zits go away before the eighth-grade dance.

My prayers with cancer were just one-sentence smoke signals:

- Please let me keep the eyebrows and the pubes.
- Please let me make it to the toilet in time.
- Please let me keep a brave face in front of the boys.

- Please keep my voice from cracking when I ask the doctor for my prognosis.

- Please keep this from bankrupting us.

- Please, if there's a hell, send every last insurance company there.

- Please, if there's not a hell, create one and send every last insurance company there.

- Please don't have the decently attractive nurse-practitioner who's about my age ask to see my hemorrhoids (an awesome chemo side effect).

Busted up and sick with cancer, the closest I could muster to anything near an actual prayer was prayer for others. Like the one I muttered under my breath for the old guy in the waiting room at the oncologist's office. He wore a herringbone blazer, a pocket square, and a boutonniere, and he was there, I overheard, by mistake. The doctor had decided to discontinue his treatment. The old man apparently didn't get the message until he got a few seats away from me.

I managed a prayer for the kid with leukemia who rode the elevator up with me one Sunday morning, both of us to receive our Neulasta injections, meant to spur the growth of our white blood cells once a round of chemo was complete. The boy's age (thirteen? sixteen? twenty-one?) was impossible to determine with no hair, facial or otherwise, on him.

I know you likely expect a clergyman to confess that cancer, with its attendant aches and terrors, deepened my prayer life.

Carrying my cross.

Belly of the whale.

Dark night of my soul.

Et cetera.

Nope.

In fact, the prayer I kept coming back to, the prayer I could say in sync with the pain and get through despite my cottony chemo-brain, was that silly prayer I learned from my great-grandma as a small child: "Now I lay me down to sleep. I pray the Lord my soul to keep. If I die before I wake, I pray the Lord my soul to take."

Fred Holly had a genuine hula girl inked on his forearm. He stockpiled for Y2K a year late, and one Sunday in Advent, he mistook my reading of Mary's Magnificat for an original sermon. Fred met the final scripture verse for the day with an applause that echoed across the mostly empty pews and said out loud, "Now, that was a good sermon, and *short*."

Fred wasn't what you'd call an intellectual guy; nonetheless, Fred's bear-embracing maxim yields still-deeper truths. The real problem with prayer when you're busted up and sick isn't that you're busted up and sick. Being busted up makes the sheer act of prayer hard, sure, but the real problem with prayer when you're stage-serious sick is the *theological* problem. Cancer, as voracious as it is rare, brings to the fore questions so obvious and so omnipresent that we often don't even see them: What's the point of prayer? Does it do anything? For what should we pray?

To put it more bluntly: Despite my degree in divinity, I found myself harboring the nagging suspicion that it was ridiculous to think of God up there in heaven to whom I could plead and who, if I was lucky or faithful enough, would hear my prayers and provide me with help.

Isn't it silly (and maybe even idolatrous), I wondered from my hospital bed, *to think that through our supplications, we can incline God a particular way, ignite one of God's passions, or persuade God into doing something God might otherwise not do?*

Cancer pulled down the covers of my unexamined beliefs and got me to consider whether prayer isn't simply a spiritually sanctioned means by which we attempt to manipulate God to do what we want. In which case, do we really believe in God or in ourselves? *Who the hell am I,* I asked myself after several stalled prayer attempts, *to think that I could manipulate God at all?*

I lost this confidence in prayer just as I lost my hair. Both losses were side effects of cancer.

Much like the drugs that managed my physical side effects, the antidote I fell upon for my spiritual side effect wasn't totally effective, but it proved adequate. I clung to an aside Paul makes in the course of his letter to the Romans. After stating the obvious (none of us knows how to pray), Saint Paul writes that whenever we pray, no matter what it might look like, it's not actually we who are praying. Rather, Paul writes, the Holy Spirit prays in us and through us. In other words, prayer isn't something we do. It's something God does; better yet, if you buy into the Trinity, it's something God shares with God. And with us. When we pray to God, we're prayed in by God.

Instead of a practice we perform for results we've predetermined, prayer catches us up into the eternal conversation Christians call Father, Son, and Holy Spirit. God is the impetus behind our prayers as much as, maybe even more than, the object of them. The very wants and desires we pray, runs Paul's argument, are themselves the handiwork of an ever-present Triune God.

What does this mean when you're sick and busted up

and trying your damnedest to pray? For one, it struck me as a refreshingly frank admission that there was no guarantee I'd be healed; when you're stage-serious sick, you hate nothing more than the empty assurances of recovery. On the contrary, it was a guarantee that my desire to be healed, as well as the desire of all those praying for me, wasn't our desire alone or even originally. It was a desire shared by—indeed, initiated by—the God who prays in us.

Which meant maybe the prayer I learned as a little child from my grandma, whom I called Nanny, was actually the best prayer of all. I'd always considered it morbid and emblematic of everything I deplore about so much of Christianity: soul-focused, death-obsessed, and heaven-directed. Yet if all prayer is rooted in and catches us up into the Father's love of the Son through the Spirit, then what could be better than to pray that we might be one day incorporated ("my soul to take") into that love?

Especially when you remember that it's not really our prayer at all.

CHAPTER 5.

AMAZING DIS-GRACE

While my prayers to keep my eyebrows were in vain and my prayers to avoid bankruptcy were still awaiting a reply, at least one of my prayers received an answer. As I neared the start of my second round of chemo, my oncologist informed me that I would not have to undergo my remaining treatments in the hospital. You should've seen my boys' faces when I tried to tell them that this was good news.

Because of the duration of chemo infusions and their intensity upon me, and because my regimen was relatively uncommon, I'd been told all along that I would have to do my chemo as an inpatient. A bigger anxiety for me even than the staggering costs of such lengthy hospital bids was worrying that my kids would not be able to visit me during those seven rounds of treatment. The compromised immune systems of the other patients on the cancer ward, I'd learned during my first round of treatment, made visits from my boys impossible as far as my nurses were concerned.

I also learned that FaceTime, when your dad's face

looks stranger by the day, is a poor substitute for in-the-flesh hand-holding.

I'd missed my youngest son's class play, which I'd foolishly promised to attend, while I was in the hospital. Later, I apologized to him one evening as I fixed his dinner. Gabriel, righteously angry with his dimples upside down in a frown, shouted at me, "I'm mad that you weren't there. You *promised*. I hate cancer. I hate that cancer has you. I hate that God makes cancer! I just wish there was no cancer."

"You'll be less likely to get an infection if you stay out of the hospital," my doctor spun the news, but I suspect he understood how urgent it was for me to be home with my kids. A few days before my second round, he told me he'd worked it out so that I would do my treatment on an outpatient basis. During the day, he explained, I would receive infusions at a stem cell center, which treated mostly leukemia patients, and then in the afternoon, the stem cell nurses would send me home with battery-powered pumps that I would hook up to my chest port in the evenings.

I soon learned to stash the wheezing pumps in my man purse and to thread the plastic tubes through the bottom of my shirt to make them less conspicuous and less likely to get caught on chairs, drawers, and doorknobs. The combination of buttons to turn the pumps on and off became a part of my muscle memory, and I soon became so adept at flushing the lines of my chest port with saline that I daydreamed about a second career in nursing.

In some ways, carrying around gallon bags of chemo-poison and bleeping pumps that looked like my boyhood Speak & Spell toy made me feel more pathetic than I had in the hospital. At least in the cancer ward, you're keeping company with other sick people. Being infused around the clock while surrounded by normal, healthy people just throws into relief how you are no longer who you were. The Christmas message that God takes on our flesh in Jesus sounds almost romantic until you find your own body revolting.

Nonetheless, the pumps allowed us to live as normal a life as possible. My boys got to see their dad. And I got to sleep with my wife. The twenty-four-hour poison pump hooked to my chest would rest between us in bed, like our baby, albeit an unwanted one. Even though the pumps prevented me from putting my arm around her and kept us from spooning our legs inside each other's as we've always done, and even though the distance the poison pump baby created between us was such that I couldn't even feel her breath blow across what was left of my chest hair, it was still more desirable than hearing, "Visiting hours are over."

As it turned out, though, I wasn't able to avoid the hospital altogether.

Chemo kills not only your cancerous cells but all your healthy, good ones, too. After each round of treatment, I'd return daily to my doctor's office for blood work, and once the numbers on my labs cratered too low, he'd send me over to the hospital, to the cancer center there, for blood transfusions. Just after my second round of treatment, I spent all of Good Friday at the cancer center, receiving multiple blood transfusions. It was the first of many days I spent there.

The previous week's chemo-poison not only killed off all my white blood cells, it eradicated most of my red blood cells too, leaving me with nosebleeds that wouldn't stop and cuts that wouldn't clot, much less heal. Where before my diagnosis, I required only the Beastie Boys' "Sabotage" on repeat to run a 5K in twenty minutes flat, this week, with my red blood running on empty, the simplest of tasks winded me so quickly it was only seconds before I could feel my heartbeat in my teeth. Worse than the shortness of breath was the anemia-induced dizziness, making me feel like a passing acquaintance was having a conversation in my head.

The irony of a preacher needing another's freely given blood on Good Friday didn't escape the staff at the cancer center. The transfusion room was a claustrophobic row of mauve recliners separated by IV poles and manila half curtains meant to create the illusion of privacy. Vinyl decals of pastel eggs and snowy Easter bunnies decorated the length of the parking-lot-view window. Though the woman sitting next to me was only about five inches from my right hand, I couldn't see her. She had a smoker's voice and swollen ankles and was wearing, I could see extending beyond the curtain's reach, worn jeans and New Balance sneakers. "The chemo's swollen me up. These are all I can get on my feet these days." I guessed she was older than me, but not by much.

She'd been talking when I sat down, and she kept on talking most of the day—as if it weren't blood that she needed. It was painful. She overshared about her private life to the staff in a way that made them blush. She told slightly inappropriate jokes to the other patients (OK, I guess that's the pot calling the kettle black). Her running commentary to the air was one long non sequitur. She offered dubious personal connections to any tidbit she heard anyone else discuss.

It felt as if we were all on a blind date and only she failed to realize how badly it was going.

She was doing anything, I quickly realized, to keep a nurse near her or a tech touching her or a stranger talking with her—even if it meant they were irritated with her. She was afraid.

By the time I was on my second unit of blood, the commentary in my head had changed from "God, she's annoying" to "She shouldn't have to be like this." By the time that second bag was bottom's up, she'd turned me introspective. I was thinking *I* shouldn't have to be like this.

I shouldn't have to be like this, I mumbled to myself. With a reflection that catches me by surprise in store windows like someone's stolen my shadow. With a face where my beard used to grow that can now go a week and still be smoother than an East German woman's bosom. With nausea that feels as familiar as a birthmark now and fingernails that feel like leaves in November.

I shouldn't have to be like this, poisoned and drained, needing blood like a washed-out vampire, with a diagnosis that made even the denizens of the cancer center regard me with equal parts pity and "but for the grace of God" relief.

GIVE ME MY BODY BACK

Maybe because it was Holy Week or maybe it was only because of the woman in the New Balance sneakers, but sitting there, I started thinking about Easter, about what Christians mean by resurrection. Sometimes I think you need less-familiar stories to drive home the why of a story so familiar it's become stock. The previous Easter, I recalled, during my children's sermon, I had decided to tell the primped and seersuckered kids the story of the seven Maccabean martyrs, one of the Old Testament's first notes of a resurrection hope. In hindsight, I should've opted to tell them about the Easter bunny.

The story, told in detail only an amateur butcher could love, is found in 2 Maccabees 7. In it, Antiochus IV Epiphanes is the most recent occupying thug oppressing the Jews. His occupying Greek regime attempts to pacify the Jews by stamping out what makes them Jews, their fidelity to Torah. In this charming little "Easter" vignette, Antiochus tries to force seven Israelite brothers and their mother, using torture, to eat pork.

Antiochus has fires built and pans and cauldrons set out for spectacle. When the first brother refuses the other white meat, Antiochus has his tongue cut out, his scalp cut off, and his hands and feet chopped off while his mom and brothers look on. Then Antiochus's troops fry him in the world's heaviest cast-iron skillet.

Thus does Antiochus do to the second brother, so the story goes, who like his elder brother refuses to forsake his faith. No sooner has Antiochus seared brother number two in a (very large) dab of butter than the third brother sticks out his tongue, freely offering it to his tormentors. Even bolder, the brother stretches out his hands and declares, in Jason's paraphrase edition: "I got these hands from the Lord, and because of his laws I forsake them, and from the Lord I hope to get them back again."

In other words: "The God in whom I've kept faith gave me this body, and God, keeping faith in me, will give it back again." God will vindicate my faithfulness. God will vindicate me.

In the text, it's a full-throated resurrection hope kind of moment, tempered only slightly by the fact that brothers four, five, six, and seven, as well as the faith-instilling matron of the family, all meet similarly grisly ends.

As you might expect, the story riveted the children when I told it to them with paschal glee. I didn't even need props. As you might also expect, some of their parents were riveted in a different sort of way. I was only about halfway through the benediction when one mother, a first-time guest, glared at me and, coming about three centimeters from my face, inquired, "What in the world kind of Easter story was *that?*"

Assuming my typical pastoral posture, I replied, in love, "Look, lady, I don't know if you've seen *Donnie Darko*, but the Easter Bunny is creepy, and besides, I'll tell you what—that story I told the kids, that's the only Easter story worth dragging our butts out of bed for on Sunday mornings."

She looked as though I'd just given her an enema. And as she dragged her two children away, I heard her say, "Yes, honey, we'll hunt for Easter eggs when we get home."

Sitting in the cancer center a year later, on Good Friday, it occurred to me that my comment to her had just been a throwaway line. It wasn't anything more than a contrarian rebuttal intended to convey that there is something greater at stake in the church's resurrection announcement than abiding her safe, civically derived sentimental expectations. But, I realized now, it's true: that story is the only Easter story worth getting out of bed every Sunday. I didn't understand how true a comment I'd uttered until I spent Good Friday getting blood.

"I got these hands from God, and because of his laws I forsake them, and from God I hope to get them back again."

God will give me my body back, says the brother.

The God who made me, one could easily paraphrase, owes me that much.

Or to put it more theologically, the God who is Goodness itself owes that much to God's own self.

As a preacher, I know better than most the extent to which our resurrection message gets watered down at Easter. While outside the church, the resurrection claim gets repackaged as springtime renewal, inside the church, we neuter the risen Jesus. We make him a symbol for our hope of life after death. Or worse, we turn Easter into the surprising coda of a grim story in which God kills Jesus with the death we deserve to die.

But if Easter is just about life after death, then the cross—a first-century electric chair—is a fucked-up symbol for a religious faith. And if Easter is merely a happy ending to a story where God's righteous system of sin accounting demands that someone die, then, frankly, God is an effed-up god, a god who, as theologian Tony Jones notes, isn't revealed in Jesus but contrasted by Jesus.

You just have to go back to that other Easter story in 2 Maccabees to see how those of us who've made resurrection about interior souls and eternal salvation have lost the plot entirely. Before resurrection is about eternal life, it's about *this* life. Easter's about vindication. In the gospel story, Easter is about the God of Israel vindicating the life of Christ by plucking him up from death for Caesar and all the world to see. Easter is the revelation—as obvious as an empty grave with an angel sitting where the imperial seal used to be—that the grain of universe, as John Howard Yoder says, runs with those who bear crosses, not build them.

Easter is about God turning the universe inside out and showing us that the seam of creation, as John says, is love. Grace and mercy. And if that's the way world runs, despite all appearances to the contrary, then damn it, eventually God will get around to vindicating those who try to live according to it.

My thoughts returned to the woman next to me in the cancer center—awkward because she's afraid, afraid because she's quite possibly dying. *She shouldn't be like this,* I thought. *Me with my MCL. Each of us with whatever keeps our lives from being the good and perfect gift God intended. The world with its manifold darkness. Things shouldn't be like this.*

God knows it. God will do something about it. That's resurrection hope. The God I've staked my life on, albeit in my imperfect way, will be faithful to me—at least I hope so.

Thanks to my Good Friday blood, by Easter my red cells were back up, and I was feeling better. But it wasn't the new blood that got me out of bed Easter Sunday. It was that resurrection hope sewn inside an unseemly story: God will vindicate me.

God will give me my body back.

CANCER DISPLACEMENT THEORY

Each time I received them, the blood transfusions made me feel better almost immediately. While the dizziness and shortness of breath remained, fresh blood made them manageable. One of the side effects of cancer, however, isn't just how you feel but how you look, and how you look, with cancer, affects how you feel every bit as much as stingy blood counts. With cancer, even on the days you feel good, you still don't look good. You look bad. You look sick. You look like you have cancer.

On the day I finished my third round of chemo, the sun was out, bright and high like a beacon leading me out of the long winter that had crashed into me. My blood counts were still up. Baseball was back, and so was I, I congratulated myself. Thanks to my recently acquired proficiency, I'd unplugged my boob tubes from my murse of chemo-poison. I was free, and I had what I so seldom did these days: an honest-to-goodness errand that had nothing to do with doctor visits, lab work, transfusions, or prescription pickups.

Well, almost. I had to deposit my disability check.

If the past few months had qualified that call-and-response cliché "God is good / All the time" for me, then that last day of my third round at least seemed the sort of day to return to old, comforting banalities. *God is good*, I said to myself in the mirror in my (I cringe as I confess) best black preacher's affectations just before snapping my fingers (both hands), spinning around, which anemic-me couldn't do all that well, and pointing at myself.

"This is the day that the Lord hath made . . . Let us rejoice and be glad in it," I declared to my mirror.

Maybe it's because my red counts were still up or I still had enough platelets pulsing through me. Maybe it was because the lymphoma was beating a retreat after my latest round, or possibly it was simply the tonic of spring. But when I looked in the mirror that day, I didn't see a five-foot seven-inch foreskin with glasses or a man-size mole rat with chest tubes attached. I saw a svelte, sexy bald dude.

It was Moby's song "Natural Blues," the cut that cribs from the single "Trouble So Hard," that played in my mind as I walked downtown that morning, wearing my slim, faded jeans (which fit once again, thanks to cancer), my Birkenstocks, and a new crisp white undershirt. I looked awesome, I thought, like James Dean after a film shoot at

Chernobyl. Not only did my doppelganger Moby supply the soundtrack for my morning, the camera for the film starring me had slowed as I walked down the sidewalk as cool as a reservoir dog. I felt good, and feeling good, I felt I looked good, too. For one brief morning at least, I was once again me. What had been lost was found. Cancer didn't have me; I had it. In check, stowed away in my back pocket with a can of whoop-ass. I. Don't. Look. Sick. At all. Or so I thought.

I started to cross the street, heading to the bank, Moby still playing in my head and reflecting off my mind's eye, when in the middle of the crosswalk, a three-foot five-inch Filipino nun, wearing a heavy navy blue habit and a crucifix around her neck large enough to crucify a fifth grader, came up to me. In the middle of the crosswalk, she grasped both my hands, as if I were about to plunge to my death. Then she said insistently, in a Spanish tinge, "I'll pray for you."

> oh lordy,
> trouble so hard
> oh lordy,
> trouble so hard,
> don't nobody know my troubles but God

And just like that, my former self-image, no matter how unmoored from reality it might have been, vanished. Like a penny and its wish, it was lost to me. God, give me my body back.

Later in my treatment, after my third or fourth round, my good friend Brian, the kind of friend whose friendship you discover is the exact definition of grace, took me to the movies one summer night. After the movie, I ducked into the men's room to wash the popcorn butter off my hands. The soap dispenser at my sink was empty. Too lazy to try the other dispensers down along the counter, I simply rinsed my hands in water and started to tear off a paper towel.

"You know you really should use soap when you wash your hands."

"Excuse me?" I asked, turning to see a teenaged theater employee at the end of the row of sinks.

"Someone in your condition," he said, "should wash good and use soap."

The crinkle in my forehead must've cried out, "My condition?!" because his face relaxed into a look of sympathy, and he added, "You have cancer, right?"

I nodded, and then so did he. Once he walked out of the bathroom, I stood in front of the line of mirrors and looked at the stranger there. And as other men drained their Big Gulp–sized sodas into the urinals, I stood behind them, my back to theirs, and cried.

The shiny Daddy Warbucks scalp, the rough cheeks hewn hairless, the waning grandma eyebrows—it was all only the outward, visible sign of what cancer does in so many inward, invisible ways. It makes you lose things.

People asked what it's like living with cancer without realizing how all the weight falls on that little preposition. Because *with* is exactly right.

The tumors take up space, psychic as much as physical, like rocks plunked down into the bucket that held your life. With nowhere else to go, other stuff—not just hair—spills out, falls by the wayside, the volume of who you used to be.

Cancer's a parasite, an intruder, a third wheel, a squatter, an unwelcome guest who rapped on the door in the middle of the night and brought more baggage than you have room.

Call it cancer displacement theory: Living with it means living without. Living with it means living with loss.

The Sunday after that little nun grasped me like an orphan in a fire, I was at the infusion center to receive the Neulasta injection that bookended my every round of chemo. A TV played *Meet the Press* on mute. Pastel Easter decorations were still taped to the tops of the IV poles that stood around the floor like silent skeletons.

Because it was the weekend, the massive market-size room of recliners and blood pressure monitors was still and nearly empty. Other than two nurses, the only person there was an old woman sitting directly across from me, a red-orange tube running from a bag to her chest. She wore a blue scarf with peacocks on it around her small, bony head. Her face looked so sunken and her skin so stretched and translucent that guessing her age felt impossible. She greeted me—exhausted, her eyes only half open—with a distinct prairie accent when I sat down and cracked open my book.

I didn't get past the first page.

She started to cry—whimper really—from the sores her chemo-poison had burnt into her mouth and tongue and throat. I'd gotten those sores, too. I felt as though I'd been skinned alive on the inside, from my tongue on down to my tailbone, so I could hardly blame her for crying as she did and then, what in any other situation would make me blush, begging, pleading with the nurse to "make the pain go away."

She kept on like that, inconsolable, with no concern

for what I or anyone else might think about her. In a different-size person you'd call it a tantrum.

When her infusion finished and her bag beeped and the nurse came to detach her port, the old woman—her whimpering a low gurgly growl now—didn't bother with the buttons on her blouse. She simply lifted up her shirt, exposing her tired-looking breasts to me.

oh lordy,
trouble so hard
oh lordy,
trouble so hard,
don't nobody know my troubles but God

It was, I can say without exaggeration, the saddest moment yet of my cancer.

Whatever dignity and decorum she'd insisted upon before in her life was gone. She no longer had room for them. Living with cancer meant living without them.

It's almost always a mistake to say when you're a pastor, but in this instance, I knew how she felt.

I'd spent every day the previous week puking in the cars of my friends, Libby and Elaine, who were kind enough to drive me back and forth from treatment. There was a time when the thought of that kind of vulnerability would've killed me. My dignity went out the window (along with my breakfast).

"Any man who would save his life must lose it," Jesus says so many times in the Gospels that I'm betting he meant it.

Only Jesus didn't mean it in the way we so often hear it. Contrary to our modern, Western preconceptions, the word *save/salvation* doesn't have anything to do with our eternal life. So it follows then that Jesus is not talking about death when speaks of loss. He's talking about losing our lives.

I was losing my ego to cancer's id.

From my perspective, Jesus was talking about losing the way your kids used to look at you before they learned to worry, losing the way they would roughhouse with you back before they considered you fragile. He was talking about losing the way you used to be able to bicker over stupid shit because you had all the time in the world, losing that embrace between you in bed where the chemo pump now goes.

He's talking about losing the recognition in the eyes of the barista who's waited on you a million times before. He's talking about losing your focus and your ability, your self-image and self-confidence, your work and the sense of usefulness it lends you. He's talking about losing your illusion that the world just couldn't go on without you.

It does. People do.

"Save" doesn't have anything to do with eternal life, so when Jesus talks about loss, it's not death he has in mind. He's talking about losing your hair, yes, and your taste and your manhood and your reliable bowel and your control over your life and your optimism over the future and your time—God, so much of your time—lost.

Maybe he's even talking about losing your ability to pray well. Maybe even—probably, I'll bet—he's thinking about losing the faith you had.

Not, losing your faith. Losing the faith you had.

> oh lordy,
> trouble so hard
> oh lordy,
> trouble so hard,
> don't nobody know my troubles but God

In the sheer boredom and down, dead time that marks so much of life with cancer, it's hard not to dwell on what you've lost and wonder what next you'll have to go without. *No matter how this goes,* I considered on many occasions, *the life we had is gone. Lost. Things are different now, and they will be different.* The string of loss was such that I wondered if we get the dynamic between faith and doubt all wrong. Or backward.

In the Eucharist, just after I hearken back to Jesus' final Passover meal with his friends in time to the stagecraft of breaking the bread and blessing the cup of wine, I declare, as the liturgy directs, the stuff of faith to be a "mystery." In like manner if in less poetry, the catechism answers that faith is possible only by grace—that is, belief in God is a gift from God, an unmerited gift. It's not, says Saint Paul, a human work. Our knowledge of and faith in God never stops being revelation, says Karl Barth; it's always a gracious act of a living God.

To wit, faith is not easily achievable.

So why, when the scriptures and the liturgies and the catechisms all direct us toward the contrary, do believers treat faith as the norm from which doubt is sometimes a retreat, rupture, or temporary break?

If belief in God can arrive only as a gift from God, then doesn't it follow that faith is more properly the stuff of sometimes? Maybe faith interrupts and intrudes upon the life of doubt. And maybe nihilism is the norm (it sure looks that way from the long end of a room filled with leukemia patients), which means that any amount of faith, for any length of moments, is a kind of miracle. A grace.

If there's any upside to so much down, I thought to myself, it's that, according to Jesus' formulation, I could expect some windfall to come my way—which is either ironic or appropriate, given that, in the gospels, the word for "save" means "healing."

Any man who would heal his life must lose it. That's what Jesus said.

MY POCKMARKED HEART

Of course, not everything that's been lost is to be lamented as loss; what's found again isn't always cause for fatted-calf rejoicing. Some things come back to you not as a homecoming but as a haunting. My mentor, Dr. Robert Dykstra, says one of the difficulties in recalling so much of childhood is not that we can't retrieve it but that what comes back to us is not welcome.

With cancer, you not only no longer look good or healthy, you don't look like you. In my case, a man.

The string of loss I experienced with cancer ushered an old, familiar shame back into my life. Midway through my treatment, Ali and I took our boys to see one of our favorite bands at our favorite family venue: the Decemberists at Merriweather Post Pavilion. When I'd bought the tickets months earlier, I'd expected to be in between chemo cycles and feeling up for a night out. Due to my increasingly sluggish recoveries, however, my treatments had gotten delayed, so I was in the middle of one of my B cycles of chemo when we drove to the concert, the tubes of my chest connected to a pump pushing a med my nurse called "Red Devil" into me. Her name for it owed either to the burning it caused in my belly or to the fact that it left my body just as red and frightening as it had entered.

By the time of the concert, I was far enough along in my chemo regimen that I was smooth and hairless. Everywhere. I was thinner too, not so much from weight loss as muscle atrophy. What my nurses called a "chemo glow" had settled over my face, giving my cheeks a warm, pink hue so that I looked like I was wearing rouge.

The cumulative effect of four rounds of chemo on my physical appearance was such that I now looked androgynous enough to play bass in an emo band.

Combine my gender-neutral appearance with the fact that on the night of the concert, a cold, rainy summer evening, I wore a decidedly feminine-looking knit cap on my head and had a blue (man) purse of Red Devil dangling from my now fey shoulder. Now picture me, at Ali's request, standing in line in the drizzle, my wife's compact flowery umbrella over my head, to order her a frozen pink sangria from a bubbling, rotating smoothie machine.

So I was surprised but perhaps you won't be to hear that the next line in this scene for which cancer had kindly set the stage was "Will that be cash or credit, ma'am?"

The band Father John Misty was just finishing their opening set behind me. Maybe I'd misheard the bartender, I prayed. Maybe she'd asked, "Will that be cash or credit, man?"

"Come again?" I squeaked, my voice cracking into a dozen different high-register decibels, none of them with any discernible notes of testosterone, which probably didn't help my case.

"Will that be cash or charge, ma'am?"

I blinked. The bartender froze, as did the sangria smoothie machine behind her. Time stopped. The rain fell languidly. The encore from the opening band gave way to the sounds of my already-cracked self-image shattering. And as though I had "the shine," I became acutely aware of every single person behind and beside me. Their eyes, I was sure, all were bearing upon me.

Oddly, I noted to myself, I felt embarrassed not only to be mistaken for a woman but to be taken, as I surely must've been, for a homely one. *Was I,* I wondered in those languid seconds, *even masculine-looking enough to pass as a butch woman? And did reflecting on such questions,* I pondered, *make me vain?*

I didn't say anything. Instead, I walked back to our seats, my head down, avoiding all the eyes I felt staring down on me. I felt exposed and wanted to die in quick anonymity under whatever rock I could find to hide beneath. I imagined the drizzle of raindrops steaming and evaporating off my hot, flushed face. I did not imagine the familiar way my body seized, both crippled and quickened with anxiety—a flinch that stretched across minutes as I realized I expected everyone around me to begin ridiculing me. I was waiting for them to shame me.

The feeling of shame instantly sent me back to a time I'd tried to forget. My anxiety turned to dread and then my dread to panic as I recalled how, no matter what I've told my kids, words hurt more than sticks and stones. And they leave more than bruises.

When I was in the sixth grade, a girl who was always introducing herself as "Candy-with-a-K" attempted to shame me one day in gym class. My newly thick and burgeoning five o'clock shadow and concomitant puberty had arrived several semesters ahead of my peers, an inauspicious development for the new kid in school.

"How many grades have you failed anyways?!" Candy-with-a-K said for all who were doing the V-sit reach to hear.

Candy-with-a-K had feathered bangs that smelled of

strawberry, rolled socks inside her Keds, and above her county-issue gym shorts, a black Guns N' Roses T-shirt with the sort of image you'd expect to see airbrushed onto the side of a conversion van.

"Look at how hairy your legs are. There's no way you're supposed to be in our grade." Candy-with-a-K looked around, hoping her comments would be like chum in the water.

Sensing the sudden need for survival, social-Darwinism style, I said, "Since you obviously like sackless, no-talent bands, I'm not surprised you don't like real men either. Guns N' Roses? Really? They're so last year."

Candy-with-a-K seemed as surprised as I was by the titters my crack set off. She blushed and hid her face behind her ample bang-age.

The riding-off-into-the-sunset version would entail Candy-with-a-K never bothering me again. I'd get the girl—any girl—and henceforth from that fateful harbinger of a day, my beard would be a source of pride, as much a part of my self-identity as Batman's cowl or Jagger's lips.

The truth is that more so than a badge of virility, my beard has always been more of a mask, covering what I'd been afraid to bare.

The premature puberty that had costumed me as a sasquatch compared with my nubile peers also ignited a four-alarm blaze of acne all over my face and body, giving Candy-with-a-K and those like her—and in junior high, who isn't like her?—more ammunition than they'd ever need to make me the kind of boiling-over loner that guidance counselors keep an eye after.

The breakouts were so severe that I hated doing anything but staying inside. Even though I didn't believe in God at the time, waking up every morning and realizing I had to go to school felt like an outright rejection of my manifold prayers and supplications. And I when I looked into the mirror each morning, I could hear the God I didn't yet believe in responding with a maniacal laugh.

My face looked worse than the "Before" pictures in the Before/After comparisons for mail-order skin meds, the craters as red and angry as I felt inside. It hurt. I used to watch Oxy commercials and daydream that my acne was only so bad. Those *Saved by the Bell* episodes where a single pimple threatens to undo a character's entire social life had the opposite effect on me. They felt like a luxuriant fantasy, positing a life for which I would've gladly traded my own.

My dermatologist, who was always dressed like a Mormon missionary, attempted to arrest my acne with an array of kitchen sink medications, including, I later discovered, a drug normally used to treat modern-day leprosy. Whether he knew it or not, it was a perceptive prescription. Though I only knew of lepers from repeated viewings of *Ben Hur* on TBS, a leper, hideous and unholy, is exactly what I felt like. I know that sounds melodramatic, but hell, it was junior high.

I was bullied every afternoon on the bus. The boys in the neighborhood would follow behind me from the bus stop as I walked home, throwing stones at me to their shouts of "zit face." I still get panicky butterflies in my stomach when I recall the afternoon that even my best friend joined them rather than, he wagered, getting singled out by them as well.

As happened to more than a few lepers, my outward affliction spread, producing in me a cynical spirit and a pockmarked heart that grew increasingly quick to search out the blemishes in others. The worst was when I'd catch my teachers trying not to stare.

CHRISTMAS WAS AN EPIPHANY

As with so many of the lepers in the Gospel stories, Jesus eventually cured me. He didn't heal me of the acne. The drugs performed that work of mercy—lots and lots of drugs. Jesus instead cured me of my self-disgust. My teacher Robert Dykstra likes to say, "To feel shame is to be in a state of absolute conviction."

Indeed, my acne compelled me to zealotry. I became a pimple-popping fundamentalist, strident in beliefs that had scabbed over and grown scars in me: that I was distasteful, that the world was a dark place, and that God, for making me and the world as we were, was a prick. Perhaps it was because of all three of these convictions or maybe just the last one that my mother one day, out of the blue, arranged for a meeting between us, God and me. "Get dressed in something nice," she said through my bedroom door, "We're going to church."

Somewhere, I'm sure, a needle scratched clear off a record. Save for a Holy Roman shotgun wedding, I'd never gone to church before. It was Christmas Eve.

From the discreet remove of the balcony, I discovered "Silent Night" had more than one verse. I dipped bread into wine, smirking at the explanation in the program: "a holy mystery." I peeked around when everyone closed their eyes and bowed their heads. I felt silly for them.

If shame puts you in a state of conviction, I think it prepares you for conviction of another kind, which I suppose is the very definition of conversion. It didn't come quickly, though. There was no altar call, and had there been one, I wouldn't have gone anywhere or given my heart to anyone. It was called a "seeker service," and in hindsight, aptly so, for I left it not converted but curious, wanting more.

Christmas was not quite an epiphany, but a word had gotten my attention that night: *incarnation*. It took root. It incarnated in me, I learned to say during the worship service. Behind that word lay a claim I hadn't heard before, one that's not so self-evident in the familiar story of Mary, Joseph, and the wise men. God takes flesh in Jesus Christ, I heard for the first time. Our flesh, the preacher preached.

God became what we are, the preacher preached in what I later learned was from Saint Athanasius, so that we can become like God.

What I was, I believed with absolute conviction, was revolting, unsightly, and therefore unlovable. My belief about my outward appearance was rendering me even uglier on the inside. To hear that God would put on my blemished skin, become what I was, take my body as God's own body—that God was as invested in my body as in my soul—wasn't a sudden wind rush of revelation, but it was disorienting. I received the notion like a puzzle piece that didn't fit the picture I'd been staring at for so long. Much like the meds my dermatologist prescribed, which took a long, unseen while to work, the idea of incarnation snuck up on me and then hibernated within me and then, much later, healed me. Or as we say in some Christian tribes, it saved me.

Eventually, incarnation became for me what the church announces it is: good news. In fact more so than a word about God's grace toward us, incarnation empowered me to show grace to myself—that is, to accept myself, just as I was, with a love I suspected I didn't deserve.

The smooth, sexless face chemo gave me was one I would've envied as a teenager, yet conversely it also awakened in me a shame and self-loathing I hadn't felt since my complexion was as eruptive as my disposition. I felt like a leper again.

In the days after my surgery, I joked often about how the "delivery" of my ample tumor baby qualified me to appreciate what women experience in childbirth. Most women, I discovered, found me neither persuasive nor funny. "C-sections go side to side, Slick, not up and down," my wife pointed out with an eye roll.

The truth is, though, if cancer didn't exactly put me in touch with my feminine side, it did unravel my masculine one.

The sangria-slinging bartender had simply stumbled on to what, up until then, I had been too ashamed to acknowledge to myself. I no longer looked or felt like a man. Or, perhaps more accurately, I'd been out of touch with what I considered masculine.

Cancer not only makes you look bad, sick all the time, it leaves you looking vague. Neutered of your former self. Feeling disgraced.

As a pastor, over the years I've had the occasion to counsel a number of women going through cancer, particularly breast cancer, so I was aware how alopecia and mastectomies can frustrate a woman's self-image. What no one bothered to prepare me for, not even the *100 Questions and Answers about Lymphoma* booklet my oncologist's office gave me, was how my cancer would mess with my sense of myself as a man. It's fair to wonder,

I suppose, whether no one warned me about it in sickness because so few men mention it in health.

The songwriter Jason Isbell, from the Drive-By Truckers, wrote a cancer song called "Elephant." It's a song about a woman who's dying, and in the way it shows instead of tells, it's slight and heartbreaking. If it were a cancer song about a man, however, I daresay the elephant in the room no one wants to face is what the disease does to a man's self-image. The hair all over my body retreated a few days ahead of my libido. My bare boy's body appeared as visible confirmation of the impotence my oncologist had speculatively raised as a possibility. The drugs that made it hard to keep food down made it next to impossible for me to get it up.

On one of the miraculous nights when my equipment seemed ready to cooperate with my tender intentions, my amour foundered against my anemia, sending my heart racing and my head spinning. In the end, the only romance I could muster was to be held and consoled over my premature dejection. I cried, which only left me feeling even less of a man.

I even had a hard time with that most mythic of masculine activities, tossing a baseball to my boys.

It wasn't until cancer robbed me of what I took to be my manhood that I began to see the amount of corrosive junk women put up with everywhere in our culture. Not seeing myself as a man, I saw for the time how women are abused by advertising at every turn, surrounded in every medium with unrealistic ideals of beauty and femininity from which they're expected to form their identity as women. I noticed too how our assumptions about manhood and masculinity are largely cobbled together from similarly insubstantial impressions.

The more I grieved the loss of my manhood, the more I sought refuge from my shame in the belief that had made me a Christian in the first place. Even as I clung to the Easter promise that God would one day give me my body back, I sought solace in the claim of incarnation: My body, even as it was, was good enough to be a flesh-and-blood vessel of the Holy, and it's that willingness of God's to take our bodies as God's own that makes them—us—holy.

What's more, it's what God does in that body that matters for how we understand ourselves as men and women, as creatures. In the incarnation, Christians say, God doesn't assume just any body or only a body, but all of our bodies. It's the most gender inclusive of beliefs. We're not only redeemed by God taking on humanity, we're represented, all of us, in God's humanity. Scripture makes this same claim narratively when, in the beginning, it declares human creatures to be made in the image of God, while later it sings of Jesus as the image of the invisible God, the firstborn of creation. Whatever it means to be a creature, therefore, what it means to be a man or a woman is to be like Jesus.

If Jesus is the prototype for humanity, then we find a proper, authentic template for ourselves not by looking to Cialis commercials, chiseled comic characters, or covers of *Cosmo*, but to the humanity embodied by Jesus in the Gospels, where we discover beauty defined by the depths of his compassion and the reach of his grace, strength displayed by restraint and sacrifice, and love blown open by vulnerability and empathy.

Carl Rogers, the influential psychologist, said the more you accept who you are, paradoxically, the more it changes you. Or as Jesus says, losing some things leads to finding others. My oncologist promised I'd get my body back—that once I completed treatment and recovered, I would return to who I was before, "just as [I was]," but I knew what he didn't.

I was different now. In small ways. For instance, without feeling embarrassed or emasculated, I can now cry.

CHAPTER 6.

NADIR

Our scars become the lessons we teach to our kids, Ryan Adams confesses in his ballad "Magnolia Mountain." The most important lessons, in other words, are the ones we'd rather not have learned. They come hard.

If there's any fruit to glean from looking stage-serious sick all the time, it's that treatment causes your pretense to fall away right along with your hair. Chemo comes upon you like a forced fast from the everyday BS by which we posture and pretend that we're better than others, that we're doing better than we are, that we have our junk together. Thus, cancer offers the lucky sufferer an extended training in keeping it real, in admitting, as the Welcome Wagon sings, "I'm not fine, and you're not fine, and we're not fine together dear."

I learned this lesson about keeping it real—or rather, I was told it—while listening to the radio in my oncologist's office one day about halfway through my treatment.

The waiting room at my oncologists' office is long and narrow, reminding me of a bus or a sound booth. I prefer the latter, I suspect, because of the small, round, raspberry-colored CD player that lies on the floor in the room. Minus the color, it's the same model my youngest son uses to listen to his *Awesome Mix Vol. 1* while he plays with his Legos.

The CD player is tucked underneath a wicker end table whose glass top itself is buried underneath stacks of "Life with Cancer" brochures and newsletters.

When I wasn't imbibing chemo-poison at the stem cell center across town, I visited this office almost every morning for lab work, dressing changes, and checkups. Sometimes my appointments were so early in the morning that I would arrive before the receptionists.

The CD player was always turned on.

Every day.

It was always already calibrated to the same DC soft-rock station, promising "the best mix of the '70s, '80s and '90s," a canard that roughly translates to "We play the same two dozen songs you heard on the radio when your babysitter drove you to Odyssey of the Mind practice in the fifth grade."

You know the radio rotation I mean: Rod Stewart's "Broken Arrow" and criminal cover of Van Morrison's "Have I Told You Lately," lots of Lionel Richie (post-Commodores), UB40's "Red Red Wine," the obligatory Whitney Houston cut, filled out by anything from Genesis (post-Peter Gabriel) or Phil Collins (pre-Disney).

When you've got cancer, I guess even "Easy like Sunday Morning" beats Wagner or, say, Morrissey.

Maybe there's a certain genius to a "best of" playlist so limited it could all fit onto one of those mix-tape cassettes I was woefully optimistic in giving to a girl in the sixth grade. Because we all—no matter our age, color, or creed—know these songs. More so even than age, color, or creed, these song unite us. Trust me, after hearing them every day at the oncologists' office, I know.

One morning, as Phil Collins sang-spoke his way through his plodding single "In the Air Tonight," all the patients in the oncologists' waiting room appeared preoccupied with their *Washington Post*s and their iPads or distracted by the dire straits ahead. Or they were until Phil Collins finally got to his ostentatious, '80s, synthesized drum solo, and six of us seated there, waiting on word of our cancer, spontaneously joined in Phil Collins's completely gratuitous drum solo, beating on our tablets and paperbacks and binder-clipped insurance claims or just making that pursed-mouth noise reserved for '80s drum effects and fight scenes in Indiana Jones movies.

Even the medical supply salesman, I spied, was tapping on his large wheeled briefcase and not so silently mouthing the words "Oh long."

A few days before that, I noticed how I wasn't the only one in the waiting room singing softly along to Extreme's cigarette-lighter-worthy single "More than Words," the slow-dance song that ended my eighth-grade year and began, I liked to think at the time, my manhood. In case you think Extreme was whiter than shopping at West Elm after watching a Focus Features movie, I was joined in Extreme's power ballad by an older black man who looked not unlike the harried cop Dad in the '90s sitcom *Family Matters.*

Several times a week in the waiting room, Billy Joel's "Piano Man" would come on the radio (God help us), and whenever it did, Paul, the real estate novelist (who never had time for a wife), was not the only one talking to Davey (who's still in the Navy). Everyone joined in with their hushed *la, la, la, la*s.

Some songs everyone knows.

One afternoon in the waiting room, I and a gruff tatted-up older man who wore his leather-worked wallet on a chain affixed to his leather-tooled belt (you know, the kind of guy you see at pawn shops or dog fights) both caught ourselves singing along to Cyndi Lauper's candy confection "Girls Just Wanna Have Fun."

When we got to the start of the chorus, he looked over at me awkwardly and shrugged. "Shit, after what this chemo's done to my testosterone, I've got as much right to sing this song as anyone else."

Then he paused and glanced down at the floor. "Sorry. Cancer kinda forces you to keep it real."

It was, I told him, the truest thing I'd heard since I got sick.

After three months of sitting in that waiting room, the soft-singing and hushed humming and toe-tapping had become so ubiquitous that I noticed when no one there was responding at all to the music—or, possibly, when some were responding too much.

Like the day when the radio played the Boss's title song from the movie *Philadelphia*, the Tom Hanks film about a losing battle with AIDS. No one sang—though I'm willing to bet everyone knew all the words as well as I do. Tom Hanks might've had a different disease, but who's to say his odds were any worse than ours? I'd wager they were all trying not to think.

Speaking of odds—

One morning I sat in the waiting room, thumbing through my Elmore Leonard novel, waiting for the nurse to call my name, when a favorite song of mine came on the raspberry radio. It was another Phil Collins song, "Against All Odds." It's quite possibly the greatest pop song of all time.

As soon as Phil Collins crooned his initial query, "How can I just let you walk away?" I could tell he had the rapt, nostalgic attention of every patient and family member in the waiting room.

And no sooner had Phil Collins gotten to his money line—the line where, in the music video, it cuts from Phil to Jeff Bridges rolling in the sand with whatshername, "You're the only one who really knew me at all"—than all of us there that morning for sticks and pricks, blood work and bad news were joining in the refrain, "So take a look at me now. . . ."

And we were all still singing, like the English-speaking world's most subdued flash mob, when we got to the end: ". . . and you coming back to me is against all odds and that's a _____.' See, you know it too.

All of us were singing or humming or whistling:

- The fifty-something businesswoman with the cane and the discourteously loud iPhone keystrokes

- The twenty-something hipster hanging on to his three-day beard, wearing a crooked Dodgers cap and an overlarge cardigan that hung down to the knees of his skinny jeans

- The sixty-something insurance-looking type with a dandruffed blazer and a mauve toupee every bit as outdated as the Palm Treo in his hand

- The lesbian couple with the matching Osprey backpacks on their laps

- And me, the erstwhile clergyman who now looked like the creepy priest in *Sin City*

All of us, clouds of varying darkness threatening over our heads, were singing about the chance you've got to take even when it's against all odds.

Thanks to the radio's best mix of yesterday, today, and tomorrow that hasn't changed since yesteryear, there are some songs that everyone just unconsciously knows, songs you can finish on your own after the shower is turned off or the car is parked or the nurse calls you back to take your vital signs.

According to Mark's Gospel at least, one of the last things Jesus does on the cross is sing: "My God, my God, why have you forsaken me?"

It's the first line from the twenty-second Psalm, a biblical song. The next line of the song sings, "Oh my God, I cry by day, but you do not answer; and by night, but find no rest."

The church typically reads Jesus' cry of forsakenness on Passion Sunday, when many are in worship, and on Good Friday, when no one is, and most often we use Christ singing this snatch of song to proof-text our interpretations of another bit of Bible music, Old Testament Isaiah's Suffering Servant songs.

When mixed into Isaiah's playlist, Jesus' cover of Psalm 22 on the cross becomes an instance of God's turning God's back on the suffering Christ.

"My God, my God, why have you forsaken me?" begins to sound as obvious as a top 40 single: God has abandoned Jesus, the vicarious sinner. Jesus on the cross is alone in the most existential possibility of the word. He's experiencing something worse than betrayal and torture and crucifixion—the sheer and total separation from God that is rightly due all of us woebegone sinners.

But "My God, my God, why have you forsaken me?" is only the first line of Israel's twenty-second song. More importantly, Psalm 22 is a song everyone in Israel would've known. As Jews, Jesus' listeners would've had all 150 psalms committed to memory. They would've sung many of them a minimum of three times a day as part of their daily office. They would've had no choice but to know the song that begins, "My God, my God, why have you forsaken me?" just as I stubbornly know all the words to Sir Mix-a-Lot's "Baby Got Back."

They could've sung Psalm 22 right along with Jesus, and maybe those near the cross that Friday did just that in the same hushed tones with which I heard a mom and her bald, thirty-something daughter sing along to Eric Clapton's "Tears in Heaven" one Friday morning in the waiting room.

Some songs everyone knows.

Jesus' listeners would've known that the song that begins with feeling forsaken ends—builds toward is more like it—on a different note entirely. The ending is faith filled and confident in God's vindication:

> For God did not despise or abhor
> the affliction of the afflicted;
> he did not hide his face from me,
> but heard when I cried to him.

So which is it?

Is Psalm 22 a Good Friday text, as we've most often made it? Or is it actually an Easter passage, foreshadowing resurrection from the dark side of the cross?

What kind of song is Jesus singing? Does he sound bruised and battered and resigned, as Springsteen does in "Streets of Philadelphia"? Or does he sound nonplussed and defiant, against all the odds, like Phil Collins?

Does Jesus, with his last bit of humanity, feel forgotten, forsaken? Or is that first line he sings meant to trigger a song in the collective memory and convey his faith?

TO SEE CHRIST IS TO SEE HIS ABSENCE

I started wondering about the song, the psalm, when a couple of days into my fifth round of chemo-poison, the nurse-practitioner, while handing me my most recent blood work, sent my already nauseous stomach for a roll: ". . . so it could just be a quirk of how your body's responding to the chemo, or it could mean the cancer's worsened in your bone marrow."

She was speculating on why my blood counts, particularly my platelet and white blood cells, were "abnormally sluggish" to recover from each round of treatment.

I gulped.

Audibly.

And looked up from the printout.

"Of course . . . there's no way to know for certain until you have a PET scan later."

Like a dirty Band-Aid, cancer pulls away the veneer from what you knew already in the basement closet of your mind. It keeps it real: Life is incredibly beautiful and terrifically shitty. Sometimes simultaneously, though more frequently, the two attributes are proximate and subsequent to one another.

Life, cancer reifies, is not unlike Saint Luke's Emmaus episode, a story we read in Eastertide but one, I believe, we could just as properly read on Good Friday. After all, isn't the "miracle" of having our eyes opened to Jesus' presence among us but a reminder that he's also just as often absent from us? Is not Christ's appearance in the breaking of the bread also subsequently (if not simultaneously) his disappearance?

Which means every sacrament, the intrusion of the holy into our world, is precious precisely because it's also at the same time a kind of exit. It's both a faith-filled, saturated moment and a forsaking—in the leave-taking sense of the word.

Life is grace and is achingly awful all at once or one right after the other in no particular order. It's feeling humbled and straight-flush lucky for the covered dishes and cards dropped at your door, but it's also feeling incredibly alone, scratching your head and wondering, self-pityingly, how people can go on with their lives when something like this is happening to *you*. It's feeling good, with halftime in your treatment within sight, and then feeling brained by a bit of—if not bad, then uncertain—news.

If every Sunday, as the church likes to say, is "a little Easter," celebrating the certainties of the resurrection, then that leaves at least one of six remaining days each week to be "a little Good Friday." To feel wronged. To feel forgotten. To feel Christ's presence vanish from you suddenly, leaving you to wonder, as those first Easter disciples did, when (or if?) he's coming back. What we might not normally prefer to admit in the pews cancer makes unavoidable: life is like that, if not for you personally, then certainly for the preponderance of people.

So that song Jesus sings from the cross—it's got to be both.

If the cross is ground zero for Jesus taking on our full humanity, the expanse of our mortal experience, then his singing the twenty-second song has got to be both—feeling faith filled and forsaken. It can't be one or the other, as our preaching typically demands of it, because our lives—the lives enfleshed in his life—are equal parts #blessed and #forsaken.

If life really is the sum of the song Jesus sings on the cross, then faith is not what so many skeptics suppose, particularly when the C-word injects a discordant note. Faith is not, as Karl Marx accused, an opiate to alleviate the pains of life. Because if life is a reliable and merciless pendulum between feeling faith filled and feeling forsaken, then to have faith is also to feel the fleetingness of faith that much more acutely. To see Christ at work in the world is to notice, even more so than those who lack faith, all the other places he is absent from the world.

Maybe that's why the ending of the Twenty-Second Psalm goes unsung or unquoted at Mark's cross. Perhaps the faith-filled notes at the end are only genuine, trustworthy, because of the feelings of forsakenness that preceded them. Maybe the author of that psalm wasn't only a good songwriter like Phil Collins. Maybe he or she was truly, fully, a no-bullshitting human, too. Just like Jesus.

There's a song, one of my favorites, by Lyle Lovett called "Fat Girl." It's not a pop song; it's definitely not the kind of song you hear on the radio. It's too brief and unromantic and bracing:

The fat girl
She always stayed inside and played piano
And she told her mother
The children made her cry
And her mother told her
They don't mean it

Now the fat girl
She ain't fat no more
And lord how she plays piano
And she sings loud
And she sings low
And she sings of love
And blind passion
But she don't mean it
She don't mean it

The fat girl, because of what she's been through, no longer
means what she says. I guess that was my biggest fear
during cancer (aside from, you know, a painful,
bankrupting, and premature death). My biggest fear was
that cancer would bring me to the point where I no longer
meant what I preached. Or prayed. Or practiced. The only
way to avoid it, I judged, was to avoid the pop pieties we
prefer and instead stick to the kind of music Jesus himself
sings—the kind that keeps it real.

CHEMO IS THE PROBLEM WITH CHEMO

If the nurse-practitioner keeping it real about how my
cancer may have worsened in my marrow brought me to
a spiritual low, then a little more than a week later, I hit a
physical low. When you have cancer, you quickly realize
how the problem with chemotherapy is that everyone
thinks chemotherapy is chemotherapy. They think
chemo is the cancer equivalent to Centrum Silver, a
catchall for every one-sized cancer customer. Whenever

someone asked me, "How's the chemo going?" I'd picture them picturing me with my chest catheter hooked up to a skull-and-cross-boned bag labeled, generically, "Cancer Drug." Or maybe, I pictured, they just pictured me swallowing it with a shot of water.

The truth is there are as many chemotherapy treatments as there are cancers, and differing intensities and durations of those treatments for all the urgencies presented by those cancers. As my oncologist put it to me after my fifth round of treatment, in the face of the latest wave of side effects, "Some chemo's not much worse than Thanksgiving with your mother-in-law, while other chemo—like yours for example—is designed to kick your fu@!^&# a$$."

Bewitched by the fact that I'm a man of the cloth, I'd sometimes wonder if it gave my doctor a titillating, confessional thrill to speak with me as though he were working on my carburetor instead of my bone marrow. Regardless of his motivation, he was dead on about the ass kicking.

The effects of the chemo-poison were cumulative, too, so with each successive round, they got worse, and each time, my recovery was like a rubber band with a little less snap than before.

Twelve days after the nurse-practitioner left me feeling forsaken, I was at my nadir. I use that term, *nadir*, not because I'm a Scrabble-playing dork but because everyone from the doctors on down to the nursing techs used it to describe my lowest low, the point following each round of treatment at which, to use my doctor's professional jargon, my butt was its most thoroughly kicked—usually about ten days after the start of chemo.

The English student in me liked that word *nadir* to

capture not just my blood chemistry but my feelings: pushed down a pendulum that wasn't swinging back. I had experienced four nadirs, and—it was no comparison—by number five, I felt at my nadir of nadirs. It was the lowest of all my lows thus far.

The first night of my fifth nadir, shivering with fever and curled up into a fetal position atop the bed, I wondered to Ali if I'd be able, physically, to make it to the end of my chemo, to come up from another four nadirs.

"This is the first time. I don't know if I can do this," I whispered.

I wasn't looking for encouragement or empathy. I genuinely didn't know if I could do it. Everything I just said about my chemo's side effects had been true this fifth go-round; ditto for the accumulating pain.

The poisons having plunged my blood counts to zero, my gums were raw and felt like they'd been treated by a plastic surgeon who dabbles in dentistry on the weekends. My tongue was swollen and covered in sores such that I couldn't swallow or speak much more than a mumble. The sores ran down my esophagus so that when I did manage to eat something it triggered this stuck-in-the-throat choking sensation. My gums, tongue, throat—they were all infected, which in turn had provoked a chronic, weeklong 100-degree fever against which my 0.01 white blood count proved no match.

To add misery to insult and injury, the chemical runs induced by the start of chemo turned to constipation. Wicked constipation. Like my colon was a character in "The Cask of Amontillado." I was fifteen pounds heavier than I had been a week previous. I was carrying around roughly twenty-one meals worth of food, plus snacks, and

I felt like someone had stuck a cork up my small intestine and then Quick Creted my ass crack for good measure.

It hurt.

CARBON-DATING MY COLON

Because my body was so vulnerable during my nadir, the dumb, stoic bravado that comes naturally to me wouldn't cut it now. I had to be forthcoming about my symptoms because, thanks to my orphaned immune system, I wasn't going to get better on my own. Whenever my temperature creeped across the 100-degree line, I was supposed to suck it up and notify the on-call oncologist, because a common cold could be enough to extradite me back to the hospital. I called him one morning during my nadir and told him about my unabated fever and my infected gums and—why not, while I've got him on the phone—the geologic layers of food frozen in my intestines.

"I'm telling you . . . it feels like I'm going to deliver a man-child. You could carbon-date some of the food that's stuck in me."

He responded with MD-worthy "hmms" to each of my complaints, and when he sensed I'd finished my rant, he asked me the question I've since learned is to health care what the question "What's in your wallet?" is to Capitol One's predatory usury: "On a scale of one to ten, how would you rate your pain?"

Doctors, nurses, phlebotomists, et al. ask that same question more than baby bird asked, "Are you my mother?"

"On a scale of one to ten, how would you rate your pain?" had been the first question that greeted me when I awoke from bowel surgery, and in the days following, it was the question against which my recuperation was measured. I was asked it at every doctor visit, every blood draw, every chemo infusion, and every platelet transfusion. The physician's assistant on the cancer advice line asked it. The nurse on the cancer ward charted it on the dry-erase board right underneath my emergency contact information. That morning, the on-call oncologist asked me it, too.

"I can't even remember the last time, it's been so long. I feel like I'm in an anus-themed version of *Alien*, except it's a much slower movie this time."

"On a scale of one to ten, how would you rate your pain?" the on-call oncologist asked me.

And I fell into the same trap I always did. I started philosophizing.

"Well, that all depends," I said as if stating the obvious.

"It depends?" he asked. I could detect the irritation blistering in his voice; for all I knew, he was clutching his iPhone on the tenth fairway.

"Yeah, it all depends. I mean, sure I feel like I'm about to deliver Shaquille O'Neal's breech love child—four weeks *late*—but it all depends on what you consider a ten. Compared with, say, the pain of dying in the Holocaust, I'm probably only a . . ."

I weighed it.

". . . a three."

He sighed, as if I'd called the on-call psychiatrist on accident.

"How high did you say your fever was?"

Just the prior morning, I had been describing how my gums felt as if they went to the prom last night with Carrie, as the nurse typed my symptoms into an Excel column labeled, I noticed, "Complaints." When I finished, she spun around on her stool and with a blank, impassive expression, she asked me that question.

"Ten being the most painful?" I asked, just to be sure.

She nodded.

"It's hard to say." And I exhaled as if class (or therapy) was finally beginning.

"Hard to say?" she repeated back to me, double-checking her English.

"Yeah, it's hard to say. It all hangs on what you consider a ten, right?"

She just stared at me.

"I mean, of course, my gums feel like someone carved them up to serve with fava beans and a nice Chianti, but compared with the pain of the world? It's gotta rate pretty low, right?"

"Huh?" she guessed.

"Have you seen the movie *Sophie's Choice*?" I asked, hoping even a clichéd tearjerker could make my point for me. She shook her head no.

"Well, Meryl Streep plays this Polish Jew during World War II, and at the end of the movie, you realize the Nazis at Auschwitz forced Sophie to choose between her two children—choose which one would live and which one would die in the ovens."

The nurse covered her mouth.

"That's horrible," she whispered as the tiniest dew of a teardrop appeared in the corner of her eye.

"I know—that's my point. It's horrible. Like, on a historic level. Can you even imagine? Something like that kind of pain has to be a ten, right? So compared with that, what kind of unweened weenie would I have to be to rank my gum pain an eight, just two shy of *Sophie's Choice*?"

"But ..."

She shook her head and blinked, as if she were only now emerging from a narcotic slumber.

"But . . . it doesn't matter, because you don't know what *Sophie's Choice* feels like yourself."

"That's just it," I countered. "You don't know what this feels like." I pointed to my gums. "So what good does my assigning an arbitrary number to it do?"

"I'll put a five down."

And she spun back around on her stool and began clacking on the keyboard.

"The doctor will be in shortly," she said.

God help him, she didn't need to say.

When you become a chronic patient, you soon discover how so much of modern medicine is premised on pain management and how it's all based on a numeracy that's about as objective as a wet dream.

"On a scale of one to ten, how would you rate your pain?" everyone asks, but the scale isn't scaled.

Compared with what? What scale are we talking about? Are these global or historic or personal proportions we're weighing? Or am I simply supposed to sort out today's gripes like a layer cake? Maybe my gums feel like Laurence Olivier is standing over me with a drill asking, "Is it safe?" but compared with having Ebola or those earthquake victims in Nepal, I'd be a pretty petty bastard to rank it higher than five. And don't even get me started on where the crucifixion should go.

It seems to me that before you ask me to plot my pain on a scale of one to ten, we should at least agree to certain benchmarks. Losing a child, let's say, is a consensus ten. Losing a spouse, meanwhile, could be a nine or a two, depending on the quality of the marriage. Childbirth, men are always being reminded, is an eight, while being hit in the nuts should never fare lower than a three. A soft tap to the nuts—the worst, as every guy knows—is always a four. We could save six for IRS audits and cavity searches, which are really just the same thing, and who would argue with paper cuts for number one?

Pain, without some mutually agreed-upon rubric, is all relative. Your ten might be the knife wounds you sustained while protecting a damsel from a mugging, but for a nancy like me, walking uphill on a hot day might be sufficient to score a seven. It's all relative.

It's all relative to me, too, to my pain. Rating the sores on my swollen tongue a five doesn't really tell you much if you don't already know that, on my pain scale, ten was reserved for the night I sat in the driveway and called Ali at work to tell her the doctor thought it might be cancer and hearing the crack in her voice as she tried not to cry.

When you're having a heart attack, you're asked if it feels like an elephant is standing on your chest. A very specific, concrete image with some heft to it. But as you recuperate from that heart attack, you'll be asked to track your pain according to a number system that feels as arbitrary as those folded-paper fortune tellers my kids make at school.

Choose your favorite color. Pick an animal. What number is your pain today?

Approaching five months of cancer under my belt, I couldn't help thinking that, rather than a smoke-and-mirrors number system, what the practice of oncology could use was a few English majors. Forget the fives and sixes that don't communicate, and rely instead upon simile and metaphor, allusion or anthropomorphism to convey your pain. I was confident, for example, that onomatopoeia would be a lot more useful to describe my diarrhea than the number three, and stream of consciousness not only has a noble lineage, it's exactly how my anemia feels.

Literary devices—that's what oncology should use.

They're the stuff of stories.

"On a scale of one to ten, how would you rate your pain?" everyone asked me as though pain were on the periodic table of common human experience.

But that's the problem: there's no such thing as common human experience. There are no universally accessible perspectives. Everything is relative. If there's one thing incarnation teaches us, it's that.

God, after all, didn't become human. God became Jesus. God didn't take on generic flesh. God took on Mary's flesh and, with it, all the stories in every knot on her family tree. God didn't become *anyone*; God became a very particular Jewish carpenter from the Ozarks of Israel.

Incarnation—that's why the numbers don't work.

The scale can't be scaled. It can't be circumscribed or universalized. Just as God cannot take on flesh without also taking on a very distinctive story, what makes us human—fully human—is not the general but the narrow, not the twos and fours but the flesh-and-blood details: "Doc, it feels as bad as the time I stuck a bat in a beehive as a boy and got stung all over me."

Each of us is as particular as the God who became the particular Jew named Jesus. Jesus does not incarnate a one-size-fits-everyone "humanity" common to us all. Rather, each of our humanities, our experiences and stories—somehow they all have a share in his unique experience and story. The scale can't be scaled. What links us together, in other words, isn't some shared, common story called the human experience. What links us together are the distinctive, particular ways we apply his unique story to our own. That's why facing cancer is a category even broader than chemotherapy and as diverse as human creatures.

During my treatment, as I got to know my fellow sufferers, I realized how we all shared a common fear—the fear of death, yes, but also the fear we wouldn't measure up to facing cancer. *What if I'm not strong enough,* we all feared, *to do this?*

If incarnation is true, however, then there's no one way to do it, no one way to face cancer. The doing it is what unites us. The same is true of following Jesus—what the church calls discipleship. There's no single right way to do it.

I got to thinking about this a lot, not just because at every turn I was asked to plot my pain along an unempirical number line. I thought about it because over those previous four months of chemo, it gradually dawned on me that I was now attempting to apply a different part of Jesus' story to my own: his death. Cancer provided an occasion for me to remember that when we're baptized, we're baptized not just for Christ's (eternal) life but into Christ's death. That's what I announce when I pour the baptismal water into the font: "So that dying and being raised with Christ, we may share in his final victory."

The manner in which we're sick, the way we handle our suffering, how we die, all the unique particulars of chemo's butt whipping—all of it are ways we live out, live up to, our baptism. Even the way in which I handled my *Around the World in Eighty Days* travel-freeze constipation.

I updated the nurse, a different one this time, about it the next morning.

"It feels like hoarders have been squatting in my colon since *Let It Bleed*."

"On a scale of one to ten, how would you rate your pain?" she asked me.

"That all depends," I said. "Have you seen *Schindler's List*?"

CHRISTIANS HAVE A COMMUNITY, NOT AN EXPLANATION

By claiming that through baptism we enter Christ's death, Christians simultaneously confess that we do not possess an explanation for suffering and evil. Instead, Christ's way of life and manner of dying give us a means to endure suffering and evil. Theologians and skeptics often put the problem into the form of a question: If God exists, then why is there so much suffering and pain in the world? Very often it's a question motivated by a deep compassion felt for the world's hurt; nonetheless, as Stanley Hauerwas points out, the assumption behind what theologians call theodicy is that God's primary attribute is power. If God existed, then God could do something about the world's suffering, the question suggests, and if God could do something about suffering, then (a good) God would do something about it.

Implicit in this assumption is another one: because humans were made in God's image, power primarily defines us as well. With such an assumption, it becomes inevitable that we would freak out and question God's existence when we lose control of our bodies or our lives. Christians, however, believe God's primary attribute is suffering love, not power—*passio*, not *potens*. Indeed

Christians profess that God's power is revealed most fully in the apparent weakness of Jesus' cross.

As a theology student and even as a pastor, I was captivated by the theodicy question in an intellectual sort of way. I could mount answers and arguments for them, but even when holding the hands of the dying, the question was never more than academic for me. It wasn't until I was down into my fifth nadir that I realized the god disproved or defended by the theodicy question isn't even the God whom I worship as a Christian. It's not the God made known in suffering love; thus, it's a god irrelevant to my suffering.

Only now that I was suffering more than I ever had in my life did I learn how Christians do not have an answer for suffering or evil. What we have, I now believe, is a community through whose compassion our faith in God is evidenced and legitimated. Our faith in the suffering love of God is intelligible, then, not through abstract answers to philosophical questions but only through the love of a community who suffer with us. Perhaps this will come as a surprise, considering I'm a clergyman, but the extent to which the community of faith is integral to the claims of faith came as an absolute shock to me.

In *The United Methodist Hymnal*, there are some songs as shallow and obvious as a commercial jingle on an AM radio station—hymns so literal and earnestly unsubtle you're half surprised when Tang and animal crackers aren't served after you're done singing them. The absolute worst among this latter group is number 558, "We Are the Church." Though its second verse sounds like the Democratic Party platform with a treble clef attached, hymn 558 merely makes the same point Mitt Romney made in the 2012 presidential campaign: corporations—I mean, churches—are people, too, my friends.

> I am the church! You are the church!
> We are the church together!
> All who follow Jesus,
> all around the world!
> Yes, we're the church together!
>
> The church is not a building;
> the church is not a steeple;
> the church is not a resting place;
> the church is a people.
>
> (Refrain)
>
> We're many kinds of people,
> with many kinds of faces,
> all colours and all ages, too
> from all times and places.

The first time I was ever asked to sing number 558, I was a new Christian and a newer undergraduate at the University of Virginia. I was worshipping at a small United Methodist church near campus. When we did a once-through of the singsong music (to "refamiliarize" ourselves), I glanced around to make sure I hadn't accidentally stepped into Vacation Bible School. Or ingested drugs.

When the schoolmarmish music director offered to demonstrate hand motions we could do along with our singing, I laughed out loud. I couldn't stop myself. And then I spent the rest of my college tenure worshipping at the Episcopal church down the street, where even if they no longer believed in God, at least they did it with style.

Not long after I became a Christian, I disliked number

558 for its tween-age verse and meter. Not long after I became a clergyman, I objected to it on a deeper level. As a minister, I recoiled at this hymn's romanticized ideals, for there's nothing quite like ministry to make you wish, every now and then, that the church were anything *but* people. After all, a brick-and-mortar building was never known to leave anonymous notes about the pastor's choice of clothes in the offering plate. A steeple has never drafted a complaint to the bishop, nor has a stained-glass window ever once challenged its pastor to a fistfight in the fellowship hall on Mother's Day. Those all really happened.

It's no secret in the United Methodist Church that every four years, hymnal committees debate the appropriateness of a hymn like "Onward, Christian Soldiers," given its violence-espousing imagery. But considering how ministry is like being nibbled to death by feral ducks, it's surprising how every quadrennium, a song like "We Are the Church" escapes the red pen.

For any song, no matter its musical merit, *how* you hear it depends on *where* you are. And it depends on your stage of life. Now that I had cancer, I could see that I'd always hated "We Are the Church" not because it's insipid (it still is), but because it's sincere. I'd mocked and hated hymn 558, and others like it, for reasons that had nothing to do with musicology or theology and everything to do with, well, me. With my heart.

I'm what you get when you mix together equal parts DNA, life experience, and Gen Y culture. Until I got cancer, I'd pretended to be cool and detached, always ironic—always, and forever feigning self-sufficiency and self-reliance, which are just unofficial adjectives for "superiority." Many in my generation are like Jane Austen characters; we're just keeping up a different pretense: cynicism. *The church can't be the people,* I'd never dared take to its logical conclusion, *because I don't need those people, and that would mean I don't need the church.* What a silly thing for a pastor to say.

Chemotherapy, as I said, eradicates not only your marrow and all attendant health but pretenses, too. When your eyebrows have gotten as thin as the blue-haired lady that sits pulpit side in the fifth pew, and when you passed out last night in the kitchen because your blood has no hemoglobin left in it, and when there's a distinct possibility your life expectancy will be shortchanged by a couple of Andrew Jacksons' worth of years, it's hard to be cool and detached. There's nothing to be ironic about. And there's no point in pretending to be self-sufficient. You, it's obvious, ain't.

Now that cancer had me back to being just a Christian and no longer a clergyman, I realized how much, as a pastor, I view Christianity as a referee, and referees aren't paid to blow the whistle in the middle of play and point out what's going right.

As a pastor, you're captured, in a good way, by who the church could be, what the church could do. But the shadow side of that vision is to notice who the church is not, what the church is not doing. Before long, you have pastors complaining how "their people" (always a fraught construction) don't pray enough, don't give enough, or don't serve enough.

To no exceptional degree, in one direction or the other, that was me, often wearing black or white but, really, acting as though I'd been ordained to wear both. And carry a whistle. However occasional or even warranted such complaining might be, it's hard for it not to calcify into cynicism. And that was me.

I don't mean to be hyperbolic. I'm not saying I was a different person by my fifth nadir or even that I'm a different person now, that cancer's changed me. I'm only suggesting that, thanks to cancer, for a time, I traded in my collar for a parishioner's shoes. I was just an ordinary Christian. Like them. And standing in their shoes, I discovered something like admiration for the people who make up the church. Only now did I appreciate, for example, how hard it is—how much trust it requires—to answer truthfully and concretely when someone asks you what are your prayer requests. That's something pastors do all the time—something I always took for granted before. That anyone does answer is, I think now, a small miracle or an act of faith of which I've been found wanting.

People outside the church often criticize, with some justification, that the church is filled with inauthentic chatter—people always talking about things that don't mean anything. There is some of that in the church, of course, but a good deal less than there is everywhere else in our lives. Now that I had cancer and I was no longer busy refereeing other people's Christianity, I realized that church people are among the only people who genuinely want an answer—and wait for it—to the question "How are you?"

Now that I was on the receiving end of the church's ministry, rather than its referee, I learned that the hardest part of accepting an offer of help, a gesture of support, or an act of compassion is accepting it. Accepting that you need it. Accepting that you (I mean, me) need these people.

All of which gets back to my problem with hymn 558, "We Are the Church," and how my problem with it was really my problem. Grace, in the jargon of the faith, isn't just a gift you do not deserve; it's a gift you didn't know you needed until you received it. This is why the gospel stories are all told from the hindsight of the resurrection, and necessarily so. You don't know how broken you are until after God has made you Easter new. Sin has no meaning until after the risen Jesus speaks, "Peace," on Easter morning.

Grace is a gift you didn't know you needed until after you received it, and in that sense, I suspect that what I've received in the midst of my lowest lows of cancer was a gift my church gives to people all the time. I just didn't realize it—or appreciate it.

The church about whom I would sometimes grouse for not praying enough or giving enough or serving enough was the same church (and by *church*, I think you've learned by now, I mean people) that texted me several times a week for prayer requests and left food at my door and organized a community run to help with the medical bills. Libby and Elaine didn't bat an eye when I barfed in their car, Brian threw my boys around in the pool because I could not, and Heather pretended not to notice (so as not to embarrass me) when I teared up when the nurse-practitioner said, "It could be because the cancer's worsened in your marrow."

One woman in my church, Gigi, sent me handwritten snail-mail cards every day—*every day*—for a year. And another, just for giggles (which are in short supply these days), persisted in posting cat pictures on my Facebook page. I don't even like cats.

Rev. Dennis Perry, the senior pastor with whom I work,

became neither my colleague nor friend but my chaplain and counselor. He was with us the night I learned I had cancer, he prayed with us the morning of my surgery, and he was there for me all during my treatment.

Cancer's funny. I'd served at this church for eleven years, and I felt like only now was I seeing who they'd been all along. And who they were, in large part, were better Christians than I. I don't even remember the moment, but my friend Brian kids me about one morning infusion when I threw up and passed out simultaneously. He caught me from hitting the floor and then wiped the vomit from my mouth, and, only semi-conscious, I apparently said to him: "I'd never do this for you. You're a much better Christian than me."

This sort of Christ-like care wasn't limited to my family of faith but extended to my family as well. My brother-in-law moved in with us to help with the kids during my treatment. And then there were my mom and my dad. I'd had a sometimes rocky, sometimes resuscitated relationship with my dad. We have a history that started when I was about the age my youngest boy is now. Even until recently, our relationship was tense and complicated—sticky, the way it always is in a family when addiction and separation are part of the story.

As with any divorce, all the relationships in the family got complicated. And as with many separations, what happens in childhood reverberates well into adulthood. A couple of years before I got cancer, I had a falling out with my mom, too. It was the kind of falling out where you can no longer remember what or who started it or if it was even important, the kind of rift that seemed to pull down every successive conversation like an undertow. The kind of argument that starts out in anger and then slowly advances on both sides toward a stubborn refusal to forgive and eventually ages into a sad resignation that this is what the relationship is now, that this is what it will be, that this thing is between us now and is going to stay there.

We had that falling out, and I'd let it fester simply because I didn't have the energy to do the work I knew it would take to repair it. And to be honest, in hindsight, I see that I hadn't had the faith to believe my relationship with either parent could be repaired.

My mom showed up the morning after I found out I had cancer. She let me know, by the way she embraced me, that the slate was wiped clean of any score we'd been keeping, and she was with us throughout my treatment. My dad, too, pushed all our past aside and showed me the sort of no-questions-asked love with which Jesus describes the prodigal's father. Both of them, my mom and my dad, made tangible the church's claim that nothing in all creation can separate us from the love of God in Jesus by their embodied insistence that (*because of the love of God in Jesus*) nothing can separate us from one another.

Every year, someone who's recently taken to reading the Bible always expresses surprise to me how much the New Testament's Easter stories are characterized by doubt and disbelief. "But some [as in not just Thomas] doubted," Matthew and Luke and John all anticlimactically testify.

But it has to be that way, I've decided since I got cancer. For the disciples, the risen Christ's wounded hands and feet can never be proof of the resurrection, because the disciples themselves are the (only) proof of the resurrection. Our faith, the truth of it, is corroborated by its end: by what it becomes in us.

And I suppose that's a better problem to have with a hymn like number 558, because the people do not just compose the church. They themselves are the proof of the church's faith by what that faith becomes in them. Like the friends who lower the paralytic down through the roof to meet Jesus, they are what my friend Thomas Lynch calls "the sacred nature of the near to hand."

CHAPTER 7.

THE LAST STRAW

My doctor's medical complex belongs to that school of architecture known as Eastern Bloc. Aside from a few teasing spaces outside, all the parking is underground. Thanks to the pre-Obamacare boom days of price-gouging health care, the complex outgrew its design long ago such that now it resembles a Lower East Side tenement building stuffed with beige medical equipment instead of rotting mattresses. On the entrance wall, the number on the fire marshal's sign announcing the building's maximum capacity might as well be whited out and instead read "Whatever" in blood-red crayon.

In a facility so crowded and busy, parking spots are as rare as erections during chemotherapy. Hours before their appointments, cars of the elderly and the ailing stalk the underground lot like walkers looking for humanity's last survivors. Indeed, it can take so long to find an empty parking spot that it's not uncommon to spot senior citizens, leaning against their walkers and siphoning gas from a parked car into their stalled-out Buick LeSabres.

After the euphoria of a found parking space settles, patients at the medical complex must tackle their next gauntlet: the elevator. To imagine what it's like waiting for the elevator in this building, first imagine the DMV.

Cross it with a TSA line where every passenger is ten minutes late for his or her flight.

Now put it in a closet.

Needless to say, having a rare, incurable cancer turned out to be a perk. On most days, I didn't need to wear my immune-deficient face mask or even say the C-word. My bald head, sunken eyes, and bare brows were enough to move me to the front of the line. Having mantle cell lymphoma was like holding a poker hand with a suicide king in it. As soon as the elevator doors dinged open, the ordinary everyday ill would part and let me pass ahead of them. More than once, after the others filled in the space around me and after the doors closed and we rose like the inverse of Jesus on Easter, the thought overwhelmed me: *I wish I were down there, with some other ailment that meant I was still waiting in line.*

One morning, having circled the parking lot for an hour, Gabriel and I were sitting in the waiting room when a heavyset woman with heather-colored bangs and a younger man, who was tall and thick, came out pushing a man I took to be her husband and his father. I recognized on the older man the chemo glow I see in the mirror. He was hunched over like a soothsayer, and his storm-colored eyes were ringed red. He'd been crying; his family still was—over something they'd been told back in the exam room, I guessed. His wife stopped directly in front of us to blow her nose, and while she did, he glanced in our direction with a faraway look, and then he nodded at me as if we were driving past each other on the same small road. Then, suddenly and quickly, he laughed.

Giggled almost. And then his son pushed him away toward the exit.

Gabriel caught more than I realized, because he clutched my arm the way he does in a storm when he's trying to squeeze his way underneath my umbrella. After the exit closed behind them, Gabriel asked me in his inside voice, "Dad?"

"Yeah, Gabriel."

"Dad, *why* do you have cancer?"

I responded, unspoken, with a question of my own: *Why is God doing this to me?*

I'd been living with the C-word for seven months, and call it professional pride, this was the first time I'd allowed myself to ask that question.

Sitting there next to Gabriel, who clung to my hairless arm, I finally asked it, finally permitted myself to step over into whatever official stage of grief is signified by such a question. Still, it was safely rendered—and kept at a remove—in the third person. The second person (Why are you, God, doing this to me?) still felt too hot to touch.

I'd never asked it myself before, but I have plenty of experience listening to that question. It comes with the job, hearing others ask that question, often followed by me reframing it.

GLENN

The first time I heard that question asked anywhere but in a movie, I'd been a seminary student for two semesters and a solo pastor for three months. A member of my tiny congregation outside Princeton, New Jersey, went home one Sunday after the ten o'clock worship service, climbed downstairs to his basement, spread out the plastic tarp that was still dirty from a long-ago family camping trip, unlocked the deer rifle with which he'd once taught his son to hunt in the Pine Barrens, sat down in a wrought-iron lawn chair, and killed himself.

His name was Glenn.

He came to church with his daughter-in-law. Sometimes her husband, his son, came with them. The son was named Glenn, too. They always sat in the very middle of the sanctuary near the center aisle.

At the end of every service, I stood outside on the steps of the church porch. He'd make his way through the line and shake my hand and say, "Nice sermon; the organ sounds out of tune, though." Then he'd walk down the sidewalk and drive away in his red PT Cruiser.

Every Sunday was like that until the Sunday he drove home and decided to take the key hidden in a kitchen coffee can and unlock his gun cabinet. Later that afternoon, his daughter-in-law called me at my apartment. And when she told me what he had done, I couldn't help myself. Without thinking how it might sound, I just asked her, "Why? Why would he do that?"

She was crying too hard to get the words out, but I heard one: *cancer*. But an answer wasn't really what I was asking for. What I wanted was something more like absolution. Because listening to her sob into the phone, I felt stabbed by guilt: guilt that I had never taken the time to get beyond "Nice sermon; the organ sounds out of tune." I was just a part-time pastor. I had books to read and papers to write and classes to attend, and he never fit into my schedule.

She caught her breath long enough to ask me if I would come over to Glenn's house.

I said yes. It wasn't until I hung up the phone that I

realized I'd never even *been* to a funeral before. Now I was going to have to perform one.

After a drive in my car that I quite honestly hoped would never end, I met them at Glenn's house. Neighbors standing in the street stared at me as I got out of the car and walked up to the house. When Glenn's daughter-in-law answered the door, I hugged her there on the front porch—not because I knew that was the right thing to do, not because I was overwhelmed with empathy or even because I'm a natural hugger. I was just terrified to say anything.

She led me down the hall to Glenn's kitchen, where we all sat down while she started to rummage through the refrigerator to make sandwiches no one would eat. Even if we couldn't articulate it, we all sensed that eating would've violated something sacred.

Sitting in Glenn's kitchen, I noticed the appointments and to-dos written on a Philadelphia Phillies calendar next to the black rotary phone on the wall. A shopping list was Scotch taped on his fridge door next to faded three-by-five photos and postcards. He needed eggs and creamer. I sat there with my hands on the pink Formica tabletop, acutely aware that my ten master of divinity courses felt like something I had mail-ordered from the back of a Marvel comic. I was in no way prepared to do what I was there to do.

Since the to-do list on Glenn's fridge door made it appear that he'd had other plans, his daughter-in-law reached for another explanation.

"Why would God do this to us?"

We sat in the quiet that was my lack of a response for a long time. Thank God we did, too. It was only later in my ministry, after I'd been with several other grieving families, that I understood how all the usual clichés we wield against death were off-limits that afternoon.

DAVID

The next time that someone asked me that question, I was sitting shotgun in a battered red F150 parked in front of the mud-brown elevation sign at the Peaks of Otter overlook on the Blue Ridge. Four thousand feet, the sign said. We were sitting in the cab of David's truck, both of us looking straight ahead, not at each other—a position I think is the only one in which men can be intimate with one another.

Looking at Bedford County below us, neither of us had spoken for several minutes until he broke the silence by asking me, "Why is this happening to me?" Which, of course, is but another way of asking, "Why is God doing this to me?"

Not long after I'd been assigned to his church, David let me know that he'd like to spend an afternoon with me. He wanted to get to know me better, he said, because he thought I'd likely be doing his funeral. David was only a few years older than I was. He'd lived every day of his life in the same small town and wouldn't have had it any other way. He'd been baptized and raised and was now raising his own two kids in the church I pastored. Ever since graduating from high school, David had worked in the local carpet factory and had served as the captain of the volunteer fire department, despite his slight frame. But when I first met him, David hadn't worked for over a year—not since his Lou Gehrig's disease had begun its monotonous mutiny against his body.

At first I'd suggested to David that we grab some lunch, but he blushed and confessed that the stiffness in his jaw and hands would make eating distracting for me and embarrassing for him. "Let's go for a drive," he suggested. He picked me up at the church. He was wearing jeans into which his wife had sewn an elastic waistband and a T-shirt that was much too big for him but was just big enough for him to be able to dress himself. I could tell he was proud that even though he could only awkwardly grip the steering wheel, he could still drive his truck.

We switched places when we got to the edge of town; he couldn't navigate the steep, winding roads that wound their way up the mountain. But we switched back again when we got to the top.

Every now and then, David would stop at places as though he were turning the pages of a family photo album. He stopped at the spot he'd gone hunting with his dad just before he died. He stopped and showed me the woods he'd snuck into as a teenager with his friends and snuck his first beer. He coasted the truck and pointed to a ridge with a clearing where he'd proposed to his high school sweetheart; he said that was the best spot to see the stars at night. And he stopped and showed me the place he liked to take his kids camping.

It was at that stop that he asked, with the V8 idling, my advice on how to tell his kids, who thus far only knew that their dad was sick, that he walked and talked funny now, not that he was dying.

David parked at the Peaks of Otter overlook and turned off the engine, and all of a sudden, the pickup took on the feel of a medieval confessional. Staring straight ahead, David faked a chuckle and told me how he'd rushed into burning homes before without a second's hesitation but that he was terrified of the long, slow death that awaited him.

He pretended to wipe away something in his eye besides a tear, and I pretended not to notice. Then he told me how he'd miss his kids. He told me he worried about them; he worried how they'd do without him.

He was quiet for a few minutes, and I knew it was coming. The question.

BETH

Not long after my drive with David, I was working double duty nearby as a hospital chaplain at the University of Virginia where one of my responsibilities was to accompany shocked and freshly grieved strangers to meet the bodies of their loved ones. I didn't need hindsight to know it was a task for which I was wholly inadequate.

One winter night, in the middle of an overnight shift, I was paged to go and meet a mother who'd arrived to see her daughter. She was waiting at the security desk when I found her; on occasions like that, they're easy to spot. She didn't look any older than my mom. Her mascara had already streaked down her cheeks and dried in the lines of her face. Her hair was matted from where her pillow had been just hours before. I noticed she hadn't put any socks on and she'd put her sweater on backward.

When I walked up to her, she had her arms crossed—like she was cold, or maybe she was holding herself. "I don't know what she was doing out this time of night," she kept whispering to herself.

A resident doctor, a med student no older than I, accompanied us. She'd been the one who'd attended her daughter when the rescue squad brought her in from the accident. The three of us walked soberly to a tiny, antiseptic room. A nurse or an orderly pulled a little chain string to draw the paper curtain open, and when the mother saw her daughter, she immediately lost her footing.

And then she lost her breath.

Then, after a long, stretched-out moment, somewhere between an inhale and an exhale, she let out a bone-racking sob. I had my arm around her to comfort her and keep her from falling, but I didn't say anything. I've always been wary of anyone who knows what to say in comfortless moments. The med student, though, was clearly unnerved by the rawness of the mother's grief and by the absence of any words. She kept looking at me, urging me with her eyes to say something. I ignored her, and the mother kept sobbing just as loudly as she'd begun.

But maybe I should've said something, because when I refused, the doctor put her hand on the mother's shoulder and looked over at the teenage girl lying on the metal bed with flecks of dried blood not all the way wiped from her hair and forehead. And the doctor said, "That's all right. She's not here. She's slipped away. That's just a shell. . . ."

I'd known instantly it was the wrong thing to say, that it rang tinny and false and was completely inadequate for the moment. Nonetheless, it surprised me when the mother pushed the doctor away and slapped her hard across the face and cried, "It's not all right. That's my daughter. She's not *just* anything. She's Beth."

Chastened, the doctor said, "I'm sorry," and slunk away.

I stayed with her a long while after that, my arm around her, listening as she stroked her daughter's hand and hair and softly recounted memories.

In all that time, she hadn't really acknowledged my presence until she turned and looked at the badge on my chest that read, "Chaplain." Then she asked me: "Why . . . why would God do this to her?"

THE *GOD'S NOT DOING THIS TO YOU* MANTRA

Those are just the memories that stick in my mind and in my craw. I've listened to some semblance of that question more times than I can recall. And over the years, I think I've acquitted myself well listening to people ask that question through tears or clenched teeth, mirroring their emotions, affirming their feelings and perspective, neither needing to protect God from their anger nor taking their anger so seriously that I turned God into a prick, all the while testifying through my compassion for them that God is *not* doing this to them.

I've even learned over the years that you don't need to be a believer to ask that question. When there is no apparent or satisfying cause to the suffering that's befallen you, believer or not, it's just a matter of time before you aim your ire at the First Cause. Where else but God does the buck eventually, eternally stop?

I still didn't know how to parse it down for Gabriel, but there was no reason, other than the obscure molecular one, that I had stage-serious cancer. So despite being practiced at exonerating God in the workplace, by my sixth round of treatment, I couldn't help but wonder why God was doing this to me. After all, God's word says that God is the one in whom my mutinous cells live and move and have their being.

Sure, I know God is not really doing this to me (I think), and I've got the diploma and the tomes to prove it, but ever since I allowed myself to ask that question, I couldn't stop wondering. I think that's what I never appreciated before, during all those times I listened to others ask the question. I never realized how once you ask that question of God, since God's not quick to answer it or allay your concerns, it just lodges there in your soul and nags away at you.

With no reason I had MCL, but every passing day of cancer, I grasped for one. My yearning for even for a bad reason was such that I couldn't look at my lab results or scan reports without scrolling down a mental list of my sins, searching for a reason, wondering if God was doing this to me because I did X to Y all those years ago.

Gabriel's question prompted a question to which I've listened more times than I can remember, and lately now, I'm listening to myself ask it. So even though I get paid to be a Christian, I found in those months that I had to repeat a sort of mantra to myself, to remind myself: *God's not doing this to you.*

When Jesus gave his disciples a prayer to pray, he first warned them, "Do not be like the pagans when you pray." The pagans believed that god—the gods—changed. The pagans believed god's mood toward us could swing from one fickle extreme to its opposite, that god could be offended or outraged or flattered by us, and that sometimes god could be for us, but other times god could be against us. So the pagans of Jesus' day would pray ridiculously long prayers, rattling off every divine name, invoking every possible attribute of god, heaping on as much praise and adoration as they could muster, in order to please and placate god. To manipulate god. To get god to be for them and not against them. The pagans believed that if they were good and prayed properly, then god would reward them, but if they were bad and failed to offer an acceptable worship then god would punish them. The pagans prayed to an auditor always tallying our ledger to bestow blame or blessing based on what we deserve, an accuser always watching us and weighing our deeds to condemn us for punishment or recommend us for reward.

The pagans had a lot of names to whom they prayed: Mars, Jupiter, Apollo. But scripture has one name for the kind of person the pagans prayed to: Satan. In the Old Testament, Satan doesn't have horns, a tail, and a pitchfork. In the Old Testament, Satan is our accuser—that's all the word means. Satan is one who casts blame upon us, who finds fault in us, who indicts us for what we deserve. Jesus doesn't want us to turn God into a kind of Satan. Jesus doesn't want us to mistake God for an accuser, to confuse God for one who casts blame and doles out what's deserved. Jesus wants us to know: the god you think is doing this to you isn't God.

God's not like that. My Father isn't like that, Jesus teaches. Our Father isn't like that. Feeling beat down and forsaken by cancer, I learned just how easy it is to be like the pagans, to turn God into a kind of Satan. So I had to remind myself: *God never changes God's mind about us—about you, Jason.* God's love does not depend on what we do or what we're like. There's nothing we can do to make God love us more, and there's nothing we can do to make God love us less.

Our sin can't change God, because God's disposition toward us doesn't change. God never gives us what we deserve and always gives us more than we deserve. God forgives even when we know exactly what we do.

No matter what it may look like in your life right now, Jason, God is for you, I'd repeat like a rosary, hoping to remind myself that I believed it.

It didn't always work.

GOD DAMN YOU, GOD

It didn't need to work all the time, though, because if the Bible is any indication, genuine, authentic faith can sometimes look and sound like despair. Rage even.

I fell upon this conviction in the weeks before my seventh round, when my nurse-practitioner commented to me, "You don't complain very much."

She had to repeat herself, because I hadn't answered the first time.

She was smoothing the cuffs of my pants, where she'd been feeling for swelling, my ankles being the primary spot my organs, exhausted from the chemo-poison, would send my body's fluid to hide.

Pretending not to know, I asked what she meant. She instructed me to lie down on the exam table and reiterated with a bit more generalizing.

"You don't ever complain."

I managed a sheepish look while she inspected my belly scar and then felt me up for swollen lymph nodes.

She stated it with such practiced neutrality that the subtext was unmistakable. It wasn't an observation; it was an indictment, a judgment: "You don't share enough." The sometimes pastoral counselor in me didn't struggle to interpret. "You don't complain" means "You're not handling this well."

She told me to sit up, and then she checked my neck, head, and armpits for lumps. After she finished, I stared blankly out the window at the overpass construction ten stories below and wondered, briefly, which vantage point—them looking up at me or me down upon them—proved a better reminder about our collective relative insignificance.

As I did, the nurse-practitioner ran down my list of side effects. "How's your light-headedness today? Your appetite? What about the numbness in your hands? Mouth sores, hemorrhoids, nausea? How are you bowels functioning? Any fevers?"

"Fine. OK. Better than before." I rattled off my answers like an understudy who's realized he'll never get to star. Preoccupied. Passionless.

She checked my eyes, I noticed, in order to catch my gaze—to make eye contact and make one more stab.

"No complaints at all?" she asked, clearly prepared to disbelieve my answer.

But I didn't give one, at least not out loud. *Little do you know*, I thought.

Since I'd last seen her, it felt as though I'd ripped off days and diary pages doing nothing but complaining. Just weeks before, I'd sat in the transplant center during my most recent round of treatment, bodysurfing a whitecap of nausea and fielding a phone call from the insurance company handling my disability leave.

This was the third or fourth such call since I'd gone on medical leave, and as on those previous occasions, I tried biting my tongue as I answered the case officer's questions about my treatment, what was behind me, and what was still before me—questions, I noted each and every time, that seemed to require an unreasonable degree of justification on my part, as if cytarabine were a Latinate alias for a Club Med to which I'd absconded on their dime.

I swallowed a shot of chemical-tasting vomit in order to get through his question, only to learn that, having finished, he had a demographic survey I was required to complete, a labyrinth of oxymoronic questions that ended, I jest not, by asking if I, Cancer Case Micheli, was right-handed or left-handed. And whether my children were right-handed or left-handed.

"They're both ambidextrous," I said, choking back my gag reflex.

That same day, after I hung up with the case officer, my nurse carried in a brown plastic bag of chemo. She held it in my lap like it was a splotchy wet newborn and asked me to confirm the name and date of birth on it as mine. I moved my lips and nodded my head and then noticed, for the first time, how underneath the patient information and the volume measurements and the polysyllabic ingredients, the brown bag carried this caution:

"Warning: Chemotherapy Drug May Cause Leukemia."

"Dumb nuts," I said in disbelief.

With the nurse, I laughed until I cried at what I called "irony"—that is, until she left the room. Then I just cried.

The truth of the matter was exactly the opposite of my nurse-practitioner' assumptions. I'd been doing nothing but complaining. A day after discovering I might beat stage-serious cancer only to contract leukemia, I spent a two-hour infusion on the phone with my insurance company, whose representative, in a twist of logic only Heinrich Himmler could appreciate, had informed me that though my oncologists were considered "in network" and thus covered by my medical policy, my doctors' equipment supplier was deemed "out of network" and thus not covered.

Another way of putting it: my treatment is paid for, so long as I pay for it.

"Wait, wait, wait," I said, flinching back a wave of queasiness, to the infuriatingly calm and euphemistically titled customer service representative. "You're telling me

I'm responsible for the type of equipment my oncologist uses?"

"Yes," she said with robotic emotion.

"So it's like a B.Y.O.S. policy," I grumbled into the phone.

"I'm sorry?" she asked, and for a second I wondered if it was actually an automated system I'd called.

"B.Y.O.S. Bring your own syringe. Or maybe B.Y.O.C.P. Bring your own chemo pump. Thank God I don't have prostate cancer. Come to think of it, maybe I should just mix up my own chemo in my bathtub like I do my gin and bring it with me to the doctor. For that matter, why do I really even need an oncologist, right? You can homeschool calculus, so why not medicine? I could just treat myself. That would be a lot cheaper for both of us, right?"

"Sir?" Her voice had managed to adopt some actual human-style feeling now.

She put me on hold, where another equally uninvested voice told me pleasantly that my call—if not my health—was being monitored for "quality assurance."

"F@#$ you," I replied sweetly to the nobody who wasn't listening on the other end and who, a few minutes later, dropped my call.

I could say that I didn't complain in the nurse-practitioner's office because it was the one place I hadn't been complaining of late, but the truth is, my nurse-practitioner being about my age and not of my gender, my biggest complaint was just too awkward to share with her.

The previous weekend, we'd taken the boys up to New York City, crossing our fingers I'd feel good enough to give them at least a small dose of a normal summer. On

Saturday, after spending the morning sailing toy boats in Central Park, we returned to our hotel room overlooking the Birdland Jazz Club on 44th Street.

At first I chalked it up to all the walking we'd done the day before. My groin hurt. It ached.

"I need to rest for a bit," I told the boys, even though I'd stood along the pond and felt myself through my linen pockets and knew. Back in the bathroom, I dropped my pants and my boxers and confirmed with my fingers what I'd felt in the park.

A lump.

In what has to be the last place a guy would choose. It was nearly as big as the two that were supposed to be there.

I held it, not really believing, for I don't know how long. And then I stared at the length of me in the mirror and saw that I was blushing—shamefaced—like you do when you're caught gawking at someone else's body, which is exactly how my body felt. I knew it was coming, so I turned on the shower hard and flicked on the overhead fan, and I started to cry—the kind where it sounds like you've been swimming for pennies in the diving well and you've just popped up for air after managing to find three.

I don't know how many minutes later, my eyes cold from the drying tears, I said sternly under my breath, "God damn it, God."

"Damn you, God."

That was only the beginning. Ministry has few job perks associated with it. Exemption from this extra indignity didn't seem too much to ask.

"This is the last straw. After everything else, this?! A lump in my dangle parts?! What are you doing—or *not* doing?" I asked like a cuckolded lover. The shower stayed on until the water ran cold.

The nurse-practitioner felt for lumps on the back of my neck and then braced both my shoulders to force me to look her in the eyes. "No complaints at all?" she asked again, forcing my eyes into hers.

But because I'm a coward by nature, I balked. "Who wants to listen to someone else complain about their problems?"

"Aren't you a priest? I mean, isn't that exactly what you do?"

"Most of them know better," I said, revealing not their feelings but my own.

Psalm 13 begins, "How long, O Lord? Will you forget me forever?" Here's another thing I know because it comes with the job: the faith displayed in the Bible bears little resemblance to the faith displayed by those who read it. Throughout their Exodus and forever after in the Promised Land, the people of Israel do not relax in elysian fields with their maker and deliverer. Instead, they perpetually wander in and out of belief in a way that puts me to mind of the permeability of the stages of grief, and as they do so, their affection for the Almighty abides a similarly fickle trajectory.

Ruth tells her remarkable story without bothering to make any mention of God. Job shakes his fist at the heavens and serves papers on God. David blames his son's death on God's tit-for-tat justice and is still too grieved to realize the rage that's due him. It's in their very identity. The name by which God calls his people into being, Israel, means "You have struggled with God and won," which is but a churchier way of saying, "You had a bone to pick with God, and you prevailed." And so often, Israel does have a bone to pick with God. Israel's father, Isaac, was named for the time his mother, Sarah, responded to a from-the-lips promise of God with a full-on belly laugh, which in my current humor I can see as an emotionally healthier response than either blind faith or bare despair.

Speaking of despair, the book of Psalms seldom sounds anything like the hymns in the pew rack or the praises sung on Christian radio. An even more jarring divergence from Israel's songs are the Hallmark cards (Sympathy Division) I've received since my diagnosis, extolling that "all things work together for good." Comforting, comfortable pieties that, in my opinion, quote just enough of God's word to risk libel.

The largest chunk of the 150 psalms do not paint pastoral scenes or spin pick-me-up bromides but are instead of the bone-picking variety. Laments, the liturgists call them.

The sentiment by which Jesus leaves this world ("My God, my God, why have you abandoned me?!") marks most of Israel's experience in the world. For every safe, buoying affirmation ("The Lord is my shepherd, I shall not want") in the book of Psalms, there are two or three cringe-worthy complaints.

Since we purpose-driven moderns have transmuted so much of the mystery of faith down to its utility (Three Biblical Steps to Success in the Workplace), it's not surprising how more often than not, our language of faith—our songs, our prayers, our cross-stitched and retweeted pieties—is meant to reassure us that, like State Farm, God is there. Our lives are in control, we assure ourselves, because (we affirm and profess and invoke and pray and petition, sing, sign, and benedict) God is in control. We can let go because we can let God. Not only did God bleed for me, God sweats the small stuff for me, too. God is my pilot or my copilot, depending upon your denominational persuasion.

Israel's language of faith, in contrast, most often spills this far more disorienting confession: our lives are exactly how they feel, out of control, because—follow the dot, dot, dot of Israel's faith logic—God is not in control. Or God is not in control in the way we'd counted on. For Israel, the result of such recognition rides the roller-coaster from anger to despair to betrayal. Laments. Complaints. Prayers that sound more like divorce decrees than love letters. Of course, it's not all bad news. A God at whom you're royally POed is not yet a God you don't believe in.

Christianity is riddled with paradoxes—the eternal made flesh, the virgin bearing a son, the dead risen—so it seems appropriate that it was just a matter of time before I found myself living one such paradox. Starting when I held myself, naked, in that hotel bathroom, I'd never been angrier in my life. I'd never felt more depressed and scared, jilted or forsaken—nor had I ever felt such self-loathing, too (what's that about, I wonder?). At the same time, though, my faith had never so closely matched the faith I find displayed in scripture as it did in those difficult months.

More and more, in my complaints I recognized myself in the Bible's psalms. My anger was more in tune with their music than the dull, accommodating, permission-seeking faith I'd held before my rage. If you'd tried to feed me some platitude about how this was one of the goods God was bringing out of ill (Genesis 50:20), that God was using cancer to deepen my faith, then, chances are, I would've punched you in the teeth. Still, it was a happening worth pondering. I was, after all, as the nurse-practitioner pointed out, a "priest," and our skills beyond such pondering are precious few.

So here's the go I made of it.

If so much of the Bible's faith takes the form of complaint, then do we, who rarely address God plainly from the bowels of our pain, preferring instead the niceties of praise and petition, commit something like unbelief?

Confessionals notwithstanding (or maybe confessionals in particular), church can be the one place where we're the least forthcoming with our actual feelings. But as I read the psalms, I wondered, *Is protecting God from the indiscretions of our hearts and tongues a graver indiscretion? Have we all colluded in implying that an ungriping attitude is a corollary to amazing grace?* Rarely are we so bald as to accuse God of what the Bible routinely accuses God: infidelity.

And once I got to pondering, I became curious about whether our reticence is itself a kind of infidelity. Thinking our holy obligation is to give God the glory, do we, in fact, rob God of glory, hugging tightly to the first draft of our testimony and offering up instead sanitized, sterilized, red-penned spiritualized jargon that intersects only tangentially with our real lives, because—we think—God's not up to the challenge of our pain or unholy emotions?

Whereas the book of Psalms is rife with dirty words and blistered emotions and impolite petitions, we most often operate as though the opposite of the familiar prayer is the case. God is the one from whom every secret may be hidden and, more so than anyone else, before whom no heart should be fully known. Which is the greater slander? Submitting to God everything of yourself, even your dirty words and ungracious anger, or submitting to God someone other than yourself? Did Job discover that those of us who refuse to curse God and die, for piety's sake, are in some sense—maybe the most important sense—already dead?

Not only does our buttoned-up language with God hide our true selves from God, it masks the real God, too. We effectively put words into God's mouth when we so selectively emphasize those few happy providential verses ("All things work together for good for those who love God") to the near exclusion of the preponderance of psalms that testify that shit happens and that God is an absentee almighty. Hiding our pain and anger from God, we often promise more than the Bible itself does—and I'm a preacher, remember, which makes me guiltier than most.

Thinking on my anger at God in those weeks and months, and reading the Psalms with eyes that never really dried, I arrived at something like a thesis statement: You only get a Bible like ours when you do not feel the need to get God off the hook. God's people could've cobbled together a far different canon. In fact, if they had, it would sell better.

You don't get a Bible like ours when you think you need to protect God from our naked emotions and most blistering of words. If you think God must be exonerated from our suffering or stood up for in the face of attack and indictments, you do not end up with a Bible like ours.

Priest that I am, I'd be remiss if I didn't note the irony that the Psalms' laments that God is MIA from our shit-happening lives are directed nevertheless *to God*. It's not so much that the psalms contend unequivocally that God is not in control of our lives, but rather the psalms are reticent to say how God is in control, and by placing them within the canon, God's people train us to be so uncertain.

It's a reluctance, I've come to believe, that requires something closer to faith than dogmatism. Faith—that is, wait-and-see trust. Of course, to feel enraged and uncertain also makes faith like an act of protest against the not-yet way of God's world. As Karl Barth, the theologian on whom I first cut my teeth, said, "To clasp the hands in prayer is the beginning of an uprising against the disorder of the world."

We pray to protest the disorder of the world, and our biggest protest is to (against?) God, who made the world and who, in Jesus Christ, promised to redeem it.

When Gabriel and I left the oncologist's office that day, after the nurse-practitioner had smoothed my cuffs and concluded I was not going to complain to her, we walked past a little girl, smaller than Gabriel, sitting in the waiting room. Her eyes looked bright in spite of her sallow complexion. She had only a few long strands of black hair left on her head, tied back nonetheless into a ponytail. She was pretending to read a flier, from a stack on the desk, advertising an upcoming 5K for cancer.

Gabriel's hand was in mine, so I didn't clasp my hands in prayer, but I did mutter a word of protest: "God damn you, God."

Only a God whose power is suffering love could appreciate the irony: faith that looks to any outsider like doubt, despair, or sometimes even rage. Perhaps this is why Jesus, before we kill him, gives us not a cross-stitched slogan about God being in control or everything happening for a reason or everything working out for good or how God won't give you more than you can handle. He gives us bread and wine—his body and blood, broken and poured out.

God, forsaken by God. Tangible reminders that whatever else we have to lament, come what may, our pain is forever joined to his. Or in the words of novelist Peter De Vries, himself no stranger to lament, having lost his daughter to leukemia: "The only alternative to the muzzle of a shotgun is the foot of the cross."

CHAPTER 8.

THE JOKE'S ON YOU

Ali blushed before she even had a grip on the sheet of paper the doctor had handed her. "Oh my," she gasped, covering her mouth as if she'd spilled a secret, "that's, um, thorough."

Ali, my mother, and I were sitting shoulder to shoulder in the mauve exam room where Dr. D— had just handed me the results of my latest PET scan. My mom read the impenetrable written summary of the findings while Ali and I looked over the scan's snapshots of my body, which included, to my surprise, the positronic outline of my man parts.

Ali blushed and laughed while I silently congratulated myself for appearing so ample in the pictures. Suddenly cancer, for giving me this shot to my self-image, didn't seem so bad.

"Let me see it." My mom reached her hand out, and reflexively, I reached mine out to cover the naughty bits in the images. "I've seen it all before," she said, rolling her eyes and grinning.

"Well, a lot's changed in thirty-five years," I said.

I'd finished my eighth and final round of chemo seven

weeks earlier. I'd staggered across the finish line like a runner who hadn't practiced on enough hills. My anemia had worsened, and with it, my constant dizziness. I'd passed out trying to do sit-ups at the gym, and I'd nearly collapsed standing in the sun at the papal mass in DC. My hands and legs were bruised from my low platelet count, which had never really recovered after my sixth and seventh rounds. And my chest port had gotten infected, turning my chest a furious, crusty red. What's more, the antibiotics the doctor had gave me to stem the infection had induced an allergic reaction, so in the days before my final round, the same nurse who'd installed the port scrubbed my infected chest with alcohol and a wire brush and then, in one long, painful motion, ripped the port out of my chest as if he were starting a lawn mower. Rather than replace it for my last round of treatment, a few days later, he installed a PICC line into my right bicep.

"So, other than my penis, what am I looking at?" I asked. The words, I noticed, quivered against my bated breath.

"You're as clear as a bell, my friend," Dr. D— said, punctuating the news with a warm, knowing smile. "All the tumors you'd had all over you," he gestured to the spots with his pen, "are completely gone."

None of us shouted hallelujah.

————————

The chemo had killed off the cancer in my body, but we all knew I could still—and likely did—have mantle cell percolating in my bone marrow, which, in the absence of the chemo drugs, would soon return lumps and masses throughout my lymph system.

So no one shouted, "Praise God!" We didn't receive the

PET scan as a miracle or proof that prayer works, but we did breathe easier than we had in almost a year. The scan wasn't unfettered good news, but it was as good as we could've hoped. If the scan had been anything but clear, then I would've had no choice but to proceed with a stem cell transplant, a procedure in which my own stem cells would be harvested from my bone marrow and treated while I received additional, and more intense, chemo. The stem cell transplant would plunge my compromised immune system even further, protracting my already slow recovery.

We'd consulted with a transplant doctor between my seventh and eighth rounds. Looking at how my recovery rates had grown slower with each successive bout of chemo, she jettisoned the medical jargon and described my marrow as "wimpy."

"At this point, I doubt we could harvest enough good stem cells from you, Jason, and I don't think, physically, you could handle the transplant process."

I'd bristled at the word *wimpy* and at the suggestion that I couldn't handle a transplant, given everything I'd already handled. "What I mean," she explained, "is that considering how slow your bone marrow has been to recover after each round of chemo, with a stem cell transplant the chance of you getting a serious infection and needing to be in isolation in the hospital for a long period of time is significant."

I might've wanted to argue about what I could handle, but she'd been right. We couldn't handle it: more sickness, more hospital time, more cancer.

Soon after school started, whether under the weight of the previous nine months or because his nine-year-old mind had finally started to comprehend the C-word,

Gabriel began to show signs of the grief and depression we'd anticipated earlier. Some nights, he cried himself to sleep, afraid he'd wake up and I would be gone. More than a few nights, we'd cried each other to sleep, both of us in our ways worried what cancer was doing to the other. Gabriel had started to tell people about Clara, his dog, who'd died, and from the franticness of the tears, you'd never guess that Clara had died years earlier.

The doctor was right. We couldn't handle what a transplant would add to our burden.

My oldest son, X, in the fall expressed bitterness that the present he'd hoped to receive for his September birthday ("your cancer being gone, Dad") was now two months overdue. Around the same time, Ali confessed to me how she couldn't keep the odds of a relapse out of her mind. "I just can't stop believing I'll be a widow by forty-five," she cried to me.

Like my marrow, we were beaten down. Gabriel needed to hear my cancer was gone. He and his brother needed to see my hair grow back, my smile and strength recover. We needed to return to our life together, even if it proved a respite rather than a new, fresh chapter.

So when my doctor announced that my scan was as clear as a bell, we didn't treat it like a loaves-and-fishes miracle, but—I suppose like the loaves and fishes—it was exactly what we needed at the time. A clear scan was just enough good news to tide us over for a while, to keep a transplant at bay.

———————

"What the scan doesn't show," Dr. D— said, scooting the little round stool closer to us, "is the level of activity of mantle cell in your marrow. We'll need to do a bone marrow biopsy for that."

The reality that the cloud of cancer would never be completely removed from my body or our lives reasserted itself and hung over us. We nodded. My mom wiped a tear threatening in the corner of her eye.

"Knowing the level of activity in your marrow will help us to gauge how we approach your maintenance chemo over the coming years."

Dr. D— offered us, each in turn, the same reassuring smile before explaining the bone marrow biopsy to us. On the back of a *Life with Cancer* newsletter, he sketched what looked like a molar; it was supposed to be my hip. Dental work, I started to suspect in that moment, might be preferable. Next to the tooth that was my hip, he drew what looked like a long syringe. The needle, I noted, was nearly twice as large as the picture of my hip.

"Is that to scale?" I asked, swallowing hard. He didn't catch my meaning.

"We'll do it here in the exam room; won't take long. We'll drill down into the center of your hip bone and extract a couple of vials of marrow."

"Come again?" I asked and maybe (my wife says no) passed out momentarily. He thought I hadn't heard him. He pointed to the cartoon and repeated himself: "We'll drill down into the center of your hip bone and extract a couple of vials of marrow."

"Did you say *drill*?!" I asked and, I could see from my reflection in the glass of the flower-print frame opposite me, blanched.

"Yes, drill," he replied obliviously.

"And am I, like, *awake* during this drilling?"

"Yes, but you needn't worry. You'll feel only a quick, momentary discomfort."

I nodded, calming down.

"I always heard it was a terrible, godawful pain," my mother, the nurse, added flatly.

"Well, I do plan on giving you a prescription for OxyContin to take before you come in that morning."

"OxyContin? I thought you said it would be only a momentary discomfort?"

He didn't reply.

"Can I just go back to having cancer?"

He slowly drew a smile across his face and then threw his head back in what seems now with hindsight less a hearty and more a diabolical laugh.

———————

I returned a week later for the bone marrow biopsy. I held out my arm for the lab nurse to draw my blood work. "I almost didn't recognize you," she said, sliding the needle into me seamlessly, "Your hair's growing back."

I brushed my goatee with my free hand. "Everyone said chemo might change the color of my hair. White wasn't what I had in mind."

"It makes you look more distinguished," she needled. "Looking distinguished is better than, you know, looking like you're dying."

"Gee, thanks." I flexed my hand as she pulled the needle out.

"It looks like I'll be back with you for your biopsy today."

"Awesome," I said and then shared with her how Dr. D— had described it as a momentary discomfort, only then to prescribe a dangerous opiate normally associated with right-wing radio hosts and gin-slinging country club wives. She smiled like a preschool teacher. "You took it, though, right?" she asked, looking suddenly sober.

"I didn't even fill it," I said. "I forgot."

"This should be . . . memorable," she said, putting a cotton swab and tape over the puncture in my arm.

"For you or for me?" I asked, the fear like diarrhea bubbling in my gut.

"Both." She was back to smiling.

"What's it feel like?"

She was putting labels on my vials of blood. "Some people scream."

"Some? What about the others?"

"They usually pass out."

"But what does it *feel* like? There's no nerves inside the bone there, so it can't hurt, right?"

She was, I could tell, thinking about something, remembering. She chuckled to herself softly, glanced over into the lab to see if her supervisor was listening, and then said, "This one guy, he said it felt like a Harry Potter Dementor sucking his soul out of his ass." I'm not sure why, but that struck me as probably the most terrifying thing she could've said.

She led me down the hallway and into the exam room. She feigned casualness, like we were on our first date and she'd just invited me upstairs to her place for a drink. "So, you can pull your pants down and lie on the table."

"Is there, like, a gown I should put on?"

"No need."

"No need for you or for me?" No response. "Where's Dr. D—?" I asked.

"He'll be along in a few minutes."

"You just need me to fold the waist of my pants down

like this, right?" I asked/prayed, pointing to the top of my hip bone underneath my belt.

"No, pull them all the way down past your butt."

Cancer is the gift that keeps on giving.

"You're lucky my butt hair hasn't grown back yet." I lamely tried to dispel the awkwardness palpable in the room. "Otherwise, you'd need to bring a Bobcat in here."

She was arranging glass specimen slides onto a metal tray. "Lucky is exactly what I was just thinking," she smirked.

Without Dr. D— there, I thought I should keep standing there, talking and chitchatting with her, even if my butt was hanging out of my pants, but with her eyebrows, she motioned for me to lie down on my belly on the butcher-paper-covered exam table.

With my face to the wall and my back to the room and my stubble-covered butt under the fluorescent lights, I hugged the institutional pillow and wished that I'd taken the OxyContin to numb me to this, if not to what was to follow. Maybe the OxyContin would've made the time pass faster, because Dr. D— didn't show for another twenty minutes. My butt started to get cold.

"Do you have plans for Christmas?" I asked the nurse. I thought about grabbing my cheeks and having my rear end do the talking like Jim Carrey in *Ace Ventura*, but somehow that didn't seem ridiculous enough for the moment. She told me about her plans to visit her grandpa, and from there we moved to swapping dinner recipes, debating whether a smoked or fried turkey was superior, discussing the merits of the new *Star Wars* film, and evaluating the off-season signings of the Washington Nationals. I found myself wondering whether she was making eye contact with me while we chatted.

After a while, a lull came to our conversation, and she grew quiet. "What are you doing back there?" I asked.

"Taking a picture."

"What?"

"You haven't seen it? We keep a corkboard in the lab of the best ones. You should feel flattered."

She snorted as Dr. D— finally knocked and rushed in. "Ah, Jason, you look well."

He said.

To my rear end.

———————

He began by feeling around on the top of my hip bone, pressing down on me with his thumb the way I do to check the doneness of a steak. What felt like bee stings followed. "Just numbing the site," he said from behind me. Next he asked the question to which *no* could be the only honest answer: "Ready?"

I squeezed the corners of the mattress. He pressed his large left hand on my back, in between my shoulder blades, pushing down on me, and grabbed a screw-shaped needle big enough to throw light off the corner of my eye. *Were it not for the American Medical Association*, I thought, *this would violate the Geneva Conventions.*

I lay my head to the side, looking away from him.

"You're going to feel a little bit of pressure," he said euphemistically as he started to twist the needle down into my bone.

"How was your Thanksgiving?" he asked.

"Fine," I grunted.

"Did you travel?"

"We went to my in-laws," I inhaled quickly and breathed out through my teeth, "in Georgia."

"Outstanding!" he announced as he bore down with his brace hand onto my upper back, trying to get more leverage. "Did you fly?"

"No, we drove."

"Oh my goodness!" he said.

"Oh my goodness is what I was just thinking," I heard the nurse giggle from somewhere behind my behind.

"How long did that take on the road?" he wondered as I wondered when the needle would pop out the other side and through my belly button.

"Twelve hours," I answered through a grimace.

"What kind of car do you drive?"

"A Bronco, but we took my wife's Subaru." I was biting at the pillow now and sweating. I was soaking wet, as I imagine all torture victims get.

"Does it get good gas mileage?"

Are you freaking serious? I thought. *Let's get this done.*

"You've got strong bones." He was grunting now. *Serves him right*, I thought.

"That's probably because I was breast-fed until I was twelve." I heard her giggle again. He did, too.

"Sorry," he said, "I need to take a break." He wiped his forehead with his sleeve. He was covered in sweat, too. The nurse squirted some water into his mouth as if he was a fighter and she was his cut man and we were still in the early rounds.

"By all means, take your time. It's not like I'm lying here with a spear screwed down into my rear end."

"I'm a briefs man myself," he declared offhandedly, apparently staring at my boxers pulled down around my knees.

"I wore my favorite pair just for you," I said.

After he spelled himself a bit, he twisted and screwed

some more. Soon after, he told me he was "in," and I then felt a tapping in the middle of me as though he were hammering on the needle with a rubber mallet. I was afraid to ask about it.

"OK, are you ready?" he asked.

"Ready? There's more?!"

"I'm going to draw the marrow out now. This might feel a bit queer."

Queer? I thought. Queer is listening to Wham!'s *Make It Big* album while drinking orange mocha Frappuccinos.

"Here we go," he said, sounding like Gene Wilder on the psychedelic chocolate-river boat.

Just then it felt like a cord was being pulled deep inside me. I could feel it inside my bones, from my heel all the way up my spine. Both of my legs kicked involuntarily, as if I were a corpse with a last bit of life in me. I blinked wide from the shock of it and tried, hard, not to cry out.

It wasn't pain exactly, but it was a feeling I never wanted to feel again. It felt, well—it felt exactly like a Harry Potter Dementor sucking my soul out of me through my ass.

"Good," he said. "Now only two, maybe three more times." I swear I smelled sulfur then and heard a maniacal laugh.

When he finished, I stood up from the exam table, too tired even to pull my pants up. "You were right about that Harry Potter thing," I said to the nurse breathlessly.

I was so sweaty that pieces of butcher paper were stuck all over my arms and face, as if I'd just had the worst shaving accident in history. "Wow," I said with astonished eyebrows, "that was the perfect way to cap off my year with cancer."

He patted me on the shoulder. "You've been through the fire, Jason."

I pulled my pants up. "Just like Shadrach, Meshach, and Abednego," I joked.

But he only stared at me blankly, the way you do at a checkout clerk whose English you can't decipher. "Yes?" he said uncertainly.

FIERY FURNACE

He should have known the story. If he didn't recall it from flannel-graphing it as a kid in Sunday school, then he should have learned it in medical school, in Oncology 101. It is, I think, a cancer story.

In the story, told in the Old Testament book of Daniel, three Jewish civil servants are denounced by King Nebuchadnezzar of Babylon for refusing to submit to the gods of Babylon and, by implication, for refusing to submit to Nebuchadnezzar. The king orders the three Jews, Shadrach, Meshach, and Abednego, to be gagged, bound, and cast into a fiery furnace—but not before he instructs his men to crank up the oven to seven times its normal heat. The furnace gets so hot that the heat obliterates the guards who come close enough to the fire to toss the prisoners inside. Not so Shadrach, Meshach, and Abednego.

According to the author of Daniel, King Nebuchadnezzar and his courtiers can see Shadrach, Meshach, and Abednego in the fiery furnace, walking around, unbound and unburned. What's more surprising, the bystanders report seeing a fourth person there in the fire: Shadrach, Meshach, Abednego, and _____?

The story in Daniel ends with a typical Old Testament

flourish when King Nebuchadnezzar, having brought Shadrach, Meshach, and Abednego out of the fire unsinged, throws off his former allegiance and declares, "There is no other god who is able to deliver in this way!" Daniel ends the story with an affirmation, but I think the story about the fire should instead end with a question. Did Shadrach, Meshach, and Abednego know? Did they see?

Certainly, they know they're alive when they didn't expect to be alive. That much is obvious. They know they've been delivered from the fire. The king makes that clear. But did they know they hadn't been alone in the fire? Did they know God had been there with them? Could they see God, feel God's presence, amidst the fire? Or could only those looking into the fire from the outside, from safety's remove, see what those inside it—in their dread and fear and pain—could not see at the time?

Having been through the fire myself, I think the answer is just as likely the latter as the former.

———————

Fire works on you like ice. It numbs you so that the pain you get used to feeling, the monotony of it, comes at the cost of not feeling much else. About Shadrach, Meshach, and Abednego I can only speculate, but the longer I was in the fire, the harder it became for me to feel God there with me, in it with me.

The truth is, if Cancer Man Jason had walked into the pastor's study sometime during the last months of my treatment, then this moderately-above-adequate pastoral counselor would have concluded that I suffered from depression. Not having enough remove on myself to diagnose well, I can at least confirm I felt exhausted:

physically, mentally, and spiritually spent from the rigors of chemo on the one hand and living with uncertainty on the other. Like Bilbo Baggins in The Fellowship of the Ring, I felt "thin, sort of stretched, like butter scraped over too much bread."

And my faith during this time?

The anger, which had marked my faith in the previous weeks, festered into a numbed absence. By absence, I don't mean I found myself no longer believing in God or no longer assenting to any of the particulars to which I was ordained. The absence I felt was one of feeling. I continued to believe in Father, Son, and Holy Spirit. Just as importantly, I continued to believe in the story named by the Trinity.

I believed my faith no less than before—in my head, I mean; but much less than before, I just didn't feel my faith—in my gut, in my heart, in my soul. The saints before us might say that I was "in the wilderness," spiritually speaking. Amputees often still feel their limbs after they're gone, but I found it's different with God. Once you feel God's gone from you, no lingering ghost of God's presence remains.

Like a lot of Protestants, I suspect, I was under the impression that "justification by faith" really meant, as theologian Robert Jenson says, that I had to save myself by the quality of my sincerity. In those last weeks in the fire, I worried that my lack of feeling God's presence was a problem, signaling a privation in me that, I subconsciously concluded, threatened the salvation of me.

I didn't feel God with me. I didn't feel my faith. And I fretted that the absence handicapped me as a first-string

Christian and, especially, compromised me as a leader of Christians.

I chewed on these worries for weeks, but then, chalk it up to the work of the Spirit or just the circuitous stages of grief, it eventually hit me. Persisting with God, even when you don't feel God, is the exact definition of faith. It's nothing other than trust.

What if Shadrach, Meshach, and Abednego prove their faith not by going into the fire but by believing Nebuchadnezzar when they're brought out it?

Not feeling God, I continued going through the motions— praying and the like—because I trusted the faith of my friends, people who testified in very ordinary ways that in such practices, God can be found. Trusting the testimony of others when you can't feel their claims for yourself is perhaps the most basic definition of faith. If I was in the desert, this turned out to be my oasis, but as is the nature of an oasis, I couldn't stay there for long. I was willing to trust what others believed for me—that God was with me in the fire—but this soon begat another fear, one with which, if I'm honest, I still struggle. *If God was most with me in the fire*, I wondered, *what would happen to my faith when I was delivered from the fire?* Cancer had proved the means by which God became a deeper reality in my heart, and I feared, crazy as it might sound, that my faith would recede once my cancer was gone.

It's the conceit of so many bad spy movies—the counter-intuitive bond between captive and captor forged by the intimacy of their shared scare. Cancer was Robert Redford to my Faye Dunaway. Cancer, like a villain, had made me a prisoner to my own body, but it had made me different, too—had brought God closer to me, even if I often required the testimony of others to believe it. And now, as I waited for the results of my bone marrow biopsy, I suffered something like Stockholm syndrome. I feared being free. Losing cancer would mean losing the immediacy of God I'd experienced with cancer.

Once Shadrach, Meshach, and Abednego heard Nebuchadnezzar's testimony about God being right there with them, close enough to touch and feel, I suspect some part of them secretly missed the fiery furnace.

MY CANCER-DIDN'T-KILL-ME-YET BUCKET LIST

I got a tattoo before I got my biopsy results.

Not always feeling my faith, and needing the faithful reminders of others, I wanted to commit onto myself a permanent reminder of what I believed but couldn't always feel. I suspect as well that, like a rash lover who commemorates his beloved by tattooing her name onto himself, I wanted some tangible sign of the complicated intimacy cancer had brought between God and me. Or maybe it was just a bucket list sort of thing.

Once I'd realized my stage-serious cancer wasn't going to kill me, at least not right away, I passed the infusion and transfusion time sketching a sort of bucket list. It's hard to sail around the world on a pastor's salary, and I've already read all the Dostoyevsky I ever want to read, so I settled upon less ambitious but no less important items for my Cancer-Didn't-Kill-Me-Yet bucket list, such as these aspirations:

3. Spend more time with friends.
7. Take my job less seriously.
2. Try to be less of a jerk to my wife.

Number six on the Cancer-Didn't-Kill-Me-Yet bucket list was something I'd always had in the back of my mind but had never gotten around to doing: getting a tattoo. I settled upon a large image of an upside-down raven, falling, with the thin outline of a cross inside it and, around the cross, the letters *B, E, A,* and *O* with compass arrows pointing out from them.

I signed my medical release and stepped through the swinging Staff Only door at the tattoo parlor. "My name's Hawk," he said, offering me his meaty orange-and-scarlet hand, tattooed with what I think were flames whose red tongues lapped seamlessly into the illustration running up his arm.

My hand disappeared into his, and I thought to myself, *Of course your name's Hawk.*

Shorter than I am, he looked like a squat version of one half of the Road Warriors, the Mad Max–inspired WWF tag team I'd idolized as a kid. Maybe Hawk was a fanboy, too, because that Road Warrior, whose signature move was to clothesline opponents from the top rope, also was named Hawk.

"Is that Hawk? Or Mr. Hawk?" I asked, like a tool. He did me the courtesy of faking a chuckle before opening the waist-high Staff Only gate and ushering me back into his studio.

Jacob, in Genesis, laid an altar to remember (and maybe warn others away from) the place where God had struggled with him. Lacking any ebenezers, I went to a tattoo parlor instead. So it was that I sat a few afternoons in Hawk's brightly animated studio, my arm draped over a vinyl cushion, sucking on lollipops to stave off the sugar crash he'd warned me the needle would provoke. It's a surprisingly intimate moment, having someone inscribe what might be a terrible mistake into your flesh. Like sex, it's sweaty and you can't take it back. And also like sex, I felt it would've been even more awkward in the absence of pillow talk. Or, in this case, banter.

No doubt I was judging, but I assumed the Republican primary or America's refugee policy would be outside his conversational wheelhouse, so I asked Hawk, "What's the strangest tattoo you ever did for someone? Please don't tell me it was a dolphin leaping through a clovered trinity or a Chinese script character that actually translates to Kick Me." But his countenance fell. He looked bothered—disturbed even. He turned off the ink gun and laid it down. Staring at the floor, he looked as though all that was missing was a fire we could gather around so he could tell this horror story. He was quiet for several moments before shaking his head and saying, "Dude, this one time, this guy had me ink this giant butterfly on his entire back."

This wasn't what I was expecting. "Well, that's not quite Flannery O'Connor," I laughed, "but that doesn't sound too strange."

"No, dude, that's not it. You see, the body of the butterfly," he looked back at the fake wood floor, "the body of the butterfly was a giant —."

Let's just say the word Hawk shared with me rhymes with *loner.*

"Seriously?" I asked him.

"Yeah, dude, and where the feet on the butterfly are supposed to go, he wanted me to put a great big pair of balls."

"Of course. It would look ridiculous without them," I deadpanned. He started to grab his ink gun but put it down again when I asked him, "Did you ask him? What was the story behind that tattoo?"

"Naw, dude. I figured it was best I didn't know."

"Probably a good call." He started again on my arm. I watched him, looking down at the upside-down *A* he had started to outline.

"This is the Alpha and Omega, right?" he asked over the whir of the gun and the Dead Weather playing over the Bose.

He must've read my "How'd you know that?" expression because he added, "We get a lot of Christians in here."

"I imagine so," I said. "I guess crosses have more staying power than the Tasmanian Devil or Calvin and Hobbes." He did me another favor by laughing.

"These here, then—this means the Beginning and the End, right?" He pointed to the other letters in the corners of the cross. I nodded, unwrapping another lollipop.

"Then this," and with the needle he outlined the crow in which the cross and letters were all contained, "must be Peter denying Jesus? The cock crowing three times? Why does it look like it's falling?" he asked, sounding genuinely curious now.

"Because while Peter's denying Jesus, Jesus is falling down, carrying his cross," I explained.

"Carrying it for Peter's sake, huh?" Hawk closed the gospel loop.

"Yeah. In a way," I said, "you can think of it as the ultimate tramp stamp."

"The three?" he asked, "the Trinity?"

"No, but that works, too. Stations of the cross, the third one."

"Why'd you decide to get a tattoo?" he asked.

"I've always wanted one," I said, grimacing at how lame that sounded, "and then cancer nearly killed me this year."

"How'd you settle on this image?" he asked, wiping the blood that was dripping down from my cross.

I sucked the lollipop spit back into my mouth. It was my turn to look at the floor.

"There's nothing like cancer and your own looming death to point out just how imperfect and unfaithful—scared and sinful—you are," I confessed. "When you're afraid you've already done most of the living you're going to do and all the important decisions you'll make in your life have already been made, you take account. And no matter how many times you count, you fear you don't measure up."

He'd stopped the ink gun again and was considering me, as I would someone in my office who'd revealed more than they knew.

"Anyway," I mumbled through the lollipop I'd returned to my mouth, "this past year I've sought refuge in the fact that, in Jesus, God takes all those experiences and emotions of ours into himself." Unintentionally saving the most important point for last, I continued, "God doesn't cause our pain and suffering. God doesn't shun us because of our shortcomings. God makes them his own. That's how we know we're not alone, because God makes all our junk his own."

And as though an affirmation, he stretched out the solitary syllable: "Duuuuuuuude."

"Yeah," I said. "I think maybe I wanted the tattoo because I've had to remind myself of it a lot this year."

He nodded as if he understood or sympathized. "So," Hawk struggled to summarize, "this basically means shit happens, but in Jesus, God shares in it with us."

I nodded. "I thought an image like this would make a better tattoo than, say, a quote like yours."

He chuckled. "You go to church?" he asked me. "You don't look the type."

"Just about every Sunday," I said.

———————

If Hawk's quote was imperfect to go on my arm, it would've been appropriate stenciled over the doorway of my doctor's office. Shit does happen, and in an oncologist's office, more often than not. But a couple of weeks after my bone marrow biopsy, when I returned to receive my results, I had my fingers crossed—and several prayer teams deployed—hoping for the "not" this time.

Dr. D— smiled at me when he entered and handed me the printout. "My friend, the mantle cell in your marrow is negligible. Congratulations."

Thank God for doctor-patient confidentiality, because I had no idea how I was supposed to react. How do you respond when you've been holding your breath for a year and you suddenly hear the best news of your life? Should you shout out with glee or jump up in the air and pump your fist, or do you chest-bump and embrace your doctor? Do you run scared, not knowing how to comprehend it, as the disciples did on resurrection morning? Do you genuflect to the holy mysteries, fall on your knees and weep, or kiss a stranger in the street?

I didn't know how I was supposed to react. The cancer movies I've seen always end like Good Friday.

My reaction was laughter.

First it was a chuckle, and then, as though the joke were just dawning on me, it became a rolling belly laugh. I laughed as if cancer was funny and the drill down into my marrow had discovered the best, most unexpected of punch lines. I laughed the way, I imagine, old, barren

Sarai must have laughed when God promised her a child—good news that strained all credulity.

No matter how I'd felt in the fire, I knew then I wasn't alone, because joy is the most infallible sign of God's presence, and despite everything, I was laughing, and really, I had been laughing plenty this whole long year.

If I were the star of my own cancer movie, this is the moment that would cue up the closing credits and the final score, with me laughing and, in a symbolic gesture, crumpling up the biopsy results into a ball and shooting it like Air Jordan into the trash can. Which is what I did.

I missed.

This was the moment when my cancer movie would end. The frame would freeze on my face mid-smile, as it does on Sundance and Butch mid-draw. My character, you'd know, was going back to his life, just as the audience members were going back to theirs. The story was finished. The nightmare was over. The Easter ending we all crave was assured.

But I knew it wasn't over. It isn't over.

As one homicide cop says to another in Richard Price's novel *The Whites*, which I'd read one afternoon in the infusion center, "What's the most bullshit word in the English language? Answer: Closure."

So I knew it wasn't over.

I knew I would still do a day of chemo every two months, maybe forever. I'd have more scans and bone marrow biopsies to monitor my status. Even though a sequel to a cancer movie would be even more disappointing than the second *Matrix* film, I knew that, on average, I had seven years until I experienced a relapse. The frame freezes on Sundance and Butch mid-draw, don't forget, to hide their unhappy ending. It wasn't over for them either.

I would have to learn how to live unafraid of what might prove inevitable. Or at least I would have to learn how to live unencumbered with the fear. It might make for a terribly boring movie, but in a sense, this is where the real story begins: learning to live without feeling like a dog chained to a stake labeled Cancer.

Even now, with every random stab of stomach pain, I find myself dwelling on the odds and the averages, knowing that this intruder lurks in me still and still will likely be the death of me.

Of course, the joke's on you. None of us is getting out of life alive.

"Thank you so much," I said in a confessional tone, after tossing the printout into the trash. "You saved my life."

"Well, you're not all the way out of the woods. There's still . . . ."

"I know," I interrupted. "I meant you saved my life—you gave it back to me—even if it's not forever."

"A lot of times, patients who've been through what you've been through realize they don't want their old life back."

"I do," I said, the truth of it stopping me. "Cancer's funny. I know it sounds lame, but I didn't realize how special my life was until this year."

I'm sure he's heard something like that a thousand times. He smiled and said, "Merry Christmas."

SPECIAL

A few nights before I got the results of my bone marrow biopsy, I was scrolling through the computer and discovering photos that, after they were snapped, had disappeared into the cloud, unseen by me. Unseen by me. Or maybe the scab always tells the truth: I was too busy to notice.

I stopped and stared at one of the photos. It was a picture of Gabriel and me, with me asleep on top of my bed and him asleep on top of my back. I cried big summer-storm teardrops when I double-clicked on it and viewed the maximized image. I didn't realize Ali had taken it. According to the date on the computer, she had snapped it on a Sunday in winter, but there's no time stamped with the date. I didn't know if this image captures an early morning after Gabriel had crawled into bed with us late on a Saturday night or if this was Gabriel having joined me for a post-worship afternoon nap. So it's a mystery. The winter light through the shades, the ratty undershirt, our exhausted faces.

The picture was taken a couple of days before that night the doctor called and asked if I was sitting down. I cried when I first saw the photo, a God's-eye image of us as innocent, happy, and—dare this preacher say it?—blessed. Even though I saw this photo during the days of waiting for my results, I don't think I would've *seen* it before.

Not the way I did now.

Mary Karr writes in Lit, "What hurts so bad about youth isn't the actual butt whippings the world delivers. It's the stupid hopes playacting like certainties."

Dr. D— likes to assure me that I'm young and healthy. I don't buy it, but I'm at least not so old that the truth of what Mary Karr says stings, because hope charading as certainty is what I saw in the picture—unexamined confidence that we have all the time in the world with each other.

And maybe we do (God, I hope we do), but I can't

pretend to be certain anymore. Even Gabriel knows that now, I think, in his way.

During my year with cancer, I did a lot of ill-advised late-night searching on Google to look up expected life spans with MCL and average remission rates and median times to first relapse. And what's so overwhelmingly tone-deaf in all the literature is how none of the facts and figures stop to consider how Ali and I have our two boys in our (wing) span. These years are ours not mine alone.

There's a word that came to mind immediately when I discovered that picture on my laptop. It's *theophany*; "a public presentation of God's immediacy" is how my fancy Bible dictionary defines it. It's God making God's self known, in the now. For instance, when God appears to Abraham and promises Abraham a future and a home and more children than the stars, God appears to Abraham as fire. That's theophany.

And when the people of Israel cross over the Red Sea, the Lord appears to them as smoke and cloud and fire and finally in an earthquake. When it's all over, the people of Israel are left promising, "We will do whatever the Lord says."

Then there's the story of Elijah. But when it comes to Elijah, God's not there—not in the wind, not in the fire, not in the earthquake. With Elijah, there's nothing. Just silence.

In the story, for the first time in his life, Elijah can't hear God all that clearly, and for the first time, this prophet doesn't know if God hears him. God's gone silent on him. So Elijah goes to the one place he can think of where he can ask God directly: Why? Why is this happening to me? Elijah goes to the place where God has spoken before, to the place where God has appeared as fire and wind and smoke and cloud and earthquake. He goes to the place where God gave Moses comfort and guidance. Elijah goes to Sinai in search of that experience—theophany.

You see, Elijah wants God to come in fire and wind and trembling. He wants God's voice to tear open the sky and speak in a boom that sweeps away all of his doubts and questions.

But what he gets is silence.

I've preached sermons on that story at least six times that I can remember, and every time I've always emphasized the silence, stressing that God's presence is found in the small, grace-filled diorama moments of our lives, not in the thunder, fire, and boom.

Looking at that picture, though, and worrying what news my biopsy would bring, I thought of that word *theophany*, and I became convinced I'd been wrong to preach it that way, because God is most assuredly in the fire and the wind and the earthquake as well the silence, lest God's not God.

A clearer way of putting it is that I think the narrator of Elijah's story is wrong, no matter his or her dramatic aim. God *is* in the fire and the wind and the tremble. After all, as God self-reveals to Moses, "I am He who Is." God, in other words, is the source of existence itself, in that everything which exists owes its existence to God. God is the answer we give to the question "Why is there something instead of nothing?" That doesn't mean God is the direct cause behind every boom, bolt, and quake, any more than every diagnosis, but as Creator, continuously holding all things in creation in existence, God is in them.

What Paul says of God and us holds true of all created things: God's "the one in whom we live and move and have our being." In all things: fire, wind, dewdrops, silence, cancerous cells.

Everything is theophany. God is in all things, necessarily, including where Elijah's narrator repeatedly stresses God is not. Richard Taylor, a philosopher, once invited readers to imagine a man who is hiking in the woods and comes upon, out of the blue, a translucent sphere. Obviously, Taylor points out, the man would be shocked by the strangeness of the object, and he'd wonder just how it should happen to be there, floating in the middle of the forest. More to the point, the hiker would never be able to swallow the notion that it just happened to be there, without cause or any possibility of further explanation. Such a suggestion would strike him as silly. But, Taylor argues (and this is money), what the hiker has failed to notice is how he might ask that same question just as well about any other object in the woods—say, a rock or a tree or a spider web or a little boy—as about this strange sphere.

He fails to do so only because it rarely occurs to us to interrogate the mysteries of the things around us. We'd be curious about a sphere suddenly floating in the forest, but as far as existence is concerned, everything is in a sense out of place.

Taylor says you can imagine that sphere stretched out to the size of the universe or shrunken to a grain of sand, as everlasting or fleeting, and it doesn't change the wonder.

What does all that mean?

It means every little detail and moment of our lives is a marvel no less than that sphere in the forest. It means every part of our lives together is a wonder of which we could ask, "Why this instead of nothing?" It means everything around us is not necessary at all, not "natural" unto itself, and as such, it's charged, all of it, with the immediacy of God. It's all graced. Back to that word again: it's all theophany.

We just seldom stop to think/notice/marvel/wonder/praise that everything from the boom and bolt to my son's morning breath against my neck is as odd, and so a gift, as that philosopher's sphere. Looking at that picture, what was obvious to me now was missed by just as wide a mark back then. We take more pictures these days but give less praise.

Cancer's funny.

Only after the fright and upheaval, the pain and the uncertainty of cancer, did I see in that still, small moment of the picture what was so clearly there. Is here. How special, as I told my doctor, my life is. Maybe it's not the case that God's not in the fire and the boom but in the silent moments, as I've always preached. Maybe the boom and the bust, the fire and the fear, calibrate our eyes to what's there all around us. All the time.

I don't know what the future will bring. I don't know if this story is over. All I know is that when I look at that picture of Gabriel and me, thinking of all the percentages and odds you can find with Google late at night, I think of that philosopher's sphere. And that word, *theophany*, makes me realize that in whatever life my family and I have left together are more marvels than we can count.

But that shouldn't keep us from trying to count them.

POST SCRIPT

When my oncologist told me for the first time "There's no cure. . . . The best we can hope for is a long remission," I read just about every cancer book I could find. I pored over them like I'd just made an unexpected career change to a job for which I was completely unqualified to perform.

One of the cancer books I read was good enough to spur me to Google the author. According to Wikipedia, he died of cancer a few years after the release of his cancer survivor memoir.

Well, crap, that's a bummer.

Who knows what end Google will yield about me in the years hence. I hope it will echo what is true for us as I write this postscript. I've returned to my work in the church and my writing at Tamed Cynic, surprised to discover there's nothing else I'd rather do. One by one, Ali and I are checking off our bucket list. Alexander's anxious hugs have abated and when I'm late picking Gabriel up from school he no longer worries it's because I've returned to the hospital.

We're back to normal(ish). Even the monthly maintenance chemo seems happily ordinary—even for my friends, James and LP, who take me to it.

As I write this, in a few weeks I will bury a man of fourscore and some years who died of Mantle Cell. More so than the stab of regret, what cancer injects into your life is perspective, as fresh as it is swift. Explain it how you will: a defect ground down deep in the DNA, the will of God, bad luck or bad karma or shit happens. Either way, just because it looks like the game of life has dealt you a piss poor card, yours can still be a winning hand. That's how we're betting these days.

If or when the sword does fall on us and the C-word again jumbles all the puzzle pieces of our lives, we'll meet that day with few meaningful regrets. If you've travelled this far into the book, then you understand what I mean when I say that's gravy.